—THE—
RESEARCH
PAPER:
SOURCES AND RESOURCES

John T. Hiers
James O. Williams
Valdosta State College

Julius F. Ariail
Georgia Southern College

D.C. Heath and Company
Lexington, Massachusetts　　　Toronto

Published simultaneously in Canada.

Printed in the United States of America.

International Standard Book Number: 0-669-07152-8

Library of Congress Catalog Card Number: 85-81378

PREFACE

The guiding principle of this book is practicality. Over the years, we have found the comprehensiveness of other guides for writing research papers to be both threatening and impractical for the beginner in composition classes. Hence, we see the need for a relatively concise, highly readable guide.

We have not attempted to illustrate every possible variable in documentation and bibliography. Nor have we tried to introduce students to every complex theoretical rationale for methodology. Our guide is designed to complement the discussions of the classroom instructors, not to eliminate them.

Consequently, we have opted for concise summary of theory. We illustrate fully only the most widely used types of documentation. Throughout we follow the format of the *MLA Handbook* (1984), but we have included the styles of the *MLA Handbook* (1980) and the *APA Publication Manual* (1983) in Chapter 7 for those who prefer it. Yet this guide does not neglect the essential elements of outlining, structuring, and developing the paper. We view the act of research writing as a process, and we endeavor to provide adequate illustration of major stages. Finally, we hope that our practical, concise approach helps to initiate the student into the satisfactions of systematic research. We hope to teach, above all, that good research is not produced in a vacuum, but that it deepens one's understanding of the ideas and events that have somehow merged to shape the lives of both individuals and cultures.

ACKNOWLEDGMENTS

We would like to thank the following reviewers for their helpful comments and suggestions: Thomas Chandler, Dekalb Community College; James Davis, University of Illinois; J. Robert Hill, Elizabethtown Community College; Louise Smith, University of Massachusetts; and Hebe Mace, Stephen F. Austin University.

We especially acknowledge with gratitude the assistance of colleagues at Valdosta State College and Georgia Southern College. Legia M. Bennett, and Rose Mary I. Foncree graciously allowed us to use and modify the fruits of their research in our sample papers. For all their support during the writing of this book we thank our families.

JTH
JOW
JFA

CONTENTS

CHAPTER 1

THE PROCESS OF RESEARCH

The research paper is a detailed study of a subject that is based on work by an individual researcher or by a group of researchers. Such research may involve tracing the history of an idea or event; it may attempt to prove a scientific hypothesis; or it may analyze trends in business. The use of research distinguishes this sort of writing from other types. An essay is usually based on the personal views of the writer concerning an idea, a social phenomenon, or a political event. A critical review allows an author to present his or her opinions or analyses concerning a work of art, literature, or music. But, a research paper requires a careful blending of personal analysis and information gleaned from sources other than the author's knowledge.

All academic disciplines require this sort of writing. While the form of the research paper may differ somewhat from discipline to discipline, the general goal remains the same: to investigate thoroughly reputable sources of information, carefully selecting, analyzing, and organizing those sources that best support the theme of the research paper. Thus, the research paper is the result of careful work. As with the essay and the critical review, a certain amount of inspiration and imagination are valuable. However, neither inspiration nor imagination can eliminate altogether the need for careful organization and examination of source information. The research writer must show knowledge of a subject by selecting the evidence, by arranging the arguments, and by clearly indicating the significance of the source information.

Unlike the essayist or the critic, the research writer does not begin work with an inspiration and a blank sheet of paper. In fact, most of the work necessary to complete a research paper should be accomplished before one attempts any writing. For beginning researchers, this preliminary work with sources and resources often pays an unexpected but pleasant dividend: the actual writing of the research paper proceeds well when the preliminaries are done correctly. However, a research paper is written, not *assembled*. It is the result of using good sources and evaluating them effectively.

The following sections of this chapter contain brief descriptions of the basic elements of research, which will be discussed in greater detail in later chapters.

Selecting a Topic

If you are selecting your own research topic, you should choose an interesting one for which research material is available. If your topic is assigned to you, be sure that you understand the nature of the subject before proceeding further. You may want to consult with your instructor. Whatever the topic, make certain that you are aware of the formal requirements for the research paper (such as length, number and type of sources, and page formats) before actually beginning work.

Narrowing the Topic

Perhaps your most difficult problem with research will be narrowing your topic. You may indeed have chosen a topic that interests you, but which is better suited for a longer work, perhaps even a book-length study. This problem sometimes occurs when you select a topic that is relatively unfamiliar. It can be remedied by general reading in the subject area.

A research paper on the subject of *inflation* would probably be unsuccessful. Libraries are crowded with information on this subject, and many information sources analyze the causes and effects of inflation throughout the economic history of the world. After sufficient reading, however, a more specific topic may suggest itself. Thus, the broad topic of *inflation* may be narrowed to *The Effects of Tariffs on Inflation* or *How the Federal Reserve Attempts to Control Inflation.* Literary topics must also be narrowed. With a little effort a research paper on Mark Twain can be narrowed to *Satire in Mark Twain's Early Journalism.*

Surveying the Literature: The Working Bibliography

With the aid of standard general reference sources (see Chapter 3), you must compile a working bibliography for your paper. The working bibliography is a list of books, magazine articles, and possibly more specialized material in pamphlets, technical reports, or government publications that will furnish the needed information. When you examine the selections in the working bibliography, you should remember that, more often than not, many of the works you chose may add to your general knowledge of the subject, but may never be documented. They may also be helpful in leading you to other, more applicable sources.

One word of caution: you should not trust your memory when you begin work with source material. In most cases you will be working with too many pieces of material to remember them all. Whatever information a source suggests, whatever ideas come to mind, you should take notes, even if all of the notes are not used later. It is most important to be systematic and accurate at this stage of your work. Avoid wasting time by needlessly having to repeat research.

The Working Hypothesis and Your Thesis

After you have surveyed the working bibliography, you will begin to determine the direction and focus of your research. In the case of the Federal Reserve's impact on inflation, for instance, you may find that, in general, the central bank's policies historically have succeeded in reducing the rate of inflation. This generalization, soundly based on the preliminary reading, may be a good working hypothesis.

The next step is to assemble additional data that narrows the working hypothesis to a thesis—a single, overriding issue or idea. For example, more research on the Federal Reserve's impact on inflation may show that during periods of high interest rates, inflation is reduced. Consequently, a thesis for the research paper begins to evolve: to curb inflation, the Federal Reserve historically reduces the money supply through higher interest rates. You may further narrow the thesis to the Federal Reserve's response to inflation in the 1970s.

Exploring the Literature

Now that you know the actual subject of your paper, you can begin going through applicable resource material on that subject to gather information that will support your specific interpretation. In addition to new sources, this process usually requires re-examination of sources discovered while you were preparing your working bibliography.

Constructing the Outline

When you have taken all of your notes, you need to outline your thoughts into a coherent presentation. Reread your note cards carefully. Then, prepare your outline, remembering to add concrete details at this early stage. As the blueprint of the paper, your outline must be thorough, logical, and exact. Outlining is a crucial stage of research. Its greatest possibilities come almost naturally, for solid, exciting research organically begins to structure itself as one idea leads to new ideas, as one relationship points to other relationships, and as one perspective illuminates several fresh perspectives. Research writing, like most other kinds of writing, is not a static, mechanical exercise. Research and writing about research begin to establish directions of their own, if allowed to. Thus, at no time is a note card, an outline, or a rough draft sacrosanct. When a new idea comes to mind from a card, a section of your outline, or from a revised paragraph, consider and nurture it. Stop and explore new ideas when they present themselves. They just might enrich the final draft of your paper.

Writing the Research Paper

After you have taken notes and have prepared an outline, you are ready to write the paper itself. You should find that the outline's pattern of headings and subheadings leads to a logical arrangement of the corresponding note cards.

Documentation

By definition, a research paper incorporates the work of other people. You must provide an accurate listing of all sources used in your own research paper. Usually this listing follows one of several standard documentary formats. Carelessness or omissions will cause your reader to suspect your ability to carry out a disciplined research project.

Some novice researchers find themselves intimidated by what they imagine is a monumental task. Indeed, individual research efforts can last for years. But, chances are that your research assignment can be completed in a matter of weeks by carefully following the procedures and guidelines recommended in this book. There is no need to be intimidated by a research task. Writing a research paper may not always be *easy,* but it is almost always *possible.*

So get started!

EXERCISES

1. List three topics that interest you or that are reasonably familiar to you.

2. Write a brief paragraph about each topic to show what makes the topic interesting.

3. Write a brief paragraph about each topic indicating the area of the topic you want to research.

4. Define *research.*

5. Define *documentation.*

CHAPTER 2

USING THE LIBRARY— WHY AND HOW

After you have decided on a preliminary form of the topic for your research paper, you should begin to look for information on that topic in your college library. As you have read in Chapter 1, your research project will give you the chance to show that you can actually locate information about a topic. As part of completing your project, you will also demonstrate that you can analyze and organize the work of other people. Of course, before you can analyze or organize your research sources, first you must select the sources from the material available in your library. But, before you can select exactly which material to use, you must be able to locate the material on your topic that is available in your library. Explaining the process of locating research materials is the purpose of this chapter.

You may be wondering why you have to bother using the library to assemble a selection of information on a certain topic, especially if you already know about your subject. One reason you have been asked to work on a research paper is that you must be able to show that you can construct a written report without being limited to your own personal knowledge.

For example, if you were a branch manager of a chain retail store and were asked by your district manager to provide the company with a report on estimated economic growth in your area, you might be able to come up with such a report based solely on your own observations of how many other businesses in your area of town are expanding their business. You might also want to include other economic indicators you have personally witnessed, such as the resale prices of homes in your neighborhood and the unemployment rate among your friends and acquaintances.

However, your company might reject your report because there is no guarantee that your personal experiences actually reflect the reality of the economic situation. To answer this request, you probably would want to read a variety of economic reports and forecasts that have been prepared by other individuals, by the Chamber of Commerce, and by state and federal government agencies. To gain access to this material, you would visit your library and plan to spend some time there.

People write books and articles on topics such as economic forecasting for two basic purposes. First, they want to record their interpretation of data. Second, they want to make their ideas available in such a way that they can be used by other people. These recorded ideas are collected and stored by the library, but the role of the library extends far beyond the collection and storage of material.

Your library can also help you locate the material you need for your research topic.

You can think of the library as an information broker, acting like a real estate broker who brings together individuals to buy and sell houses. Instead of houses, the librarian deals with information. But, just as houses come in many designs, information is available in many different packages. In the process of looking for material on your topic, you may come across encyclopedias, books, magazine articles, reports prepared by government agencies, newspaper articles, or audio-visual material such as cassettes and filmstrips.

Two Approaches to Using the Library

Before going to the library to begin work on your research paper, you might consider two preliminary ideas about using a college library. The first idea is that your library, like many gasoline stations today, provides self-service and full-service at the same time. If you need gasoline for your car, you can choose to pump it yourself or you can have a station attendant pump it for you. Similarly, if you know enough about your library to locate the necessary information by yourself, that's fine. However, if you need help locating information, then the library staff is available to help you. You can choose which method you prefer, and you can use both methods at any time.

The second idea is that it is quite possible to find the same information in several places in your library by using different techniques. For example, to answer the question, "How high is Mt. Everest?" you could take any one of the following approaches:

1. look up *Mt. Everest* in an encyclopedia article;

2. look up *World's Highest Mountains* in an almanac;

3. using the library catalog, find a book on Mt. Everest;

4. using a magazine index, find an article on Mt. Everest.

Since it is often possible to use several ways to locate the same information, most people decide on a way which is most comfortable for them and they continue with it. No one (not even a librarian) can be familiar with all of the information resources in a library, and there is no need for you to be intimidated by the mass of information available. Even if you could find the height of Mt. Everest in a hundred different sources, one or two of these sources would probably do just as well.

The Physical Arrangement of the Library

If you have the time to spend a few hours in your library before you actually have to begin work on your research paper, you should spend those hours getting acquainted with the different areas and services available to you there. You might take a tour guided by a member of the library staff, or perhaps follow a printed diagram in a self-guided tour. You might also just wander around yourself, until you feel reasonably familiar with the physical layout of the building and the types of services available to you in various locations. This process will be beneficial to you later, when you are referred by the library catalog or by the staff to material located in a certain area. If you already know where that area is, the directions will be more meaningful.

Many libraries divide the physical space inside their buildings into three main areas for service, storage, and study purposes. The service areas usually contain the reference and circulation departments, and perhaps other departments devoted to audio-visual materials or government documents. The storage areas contain the many rows of bookshelves needed to hold the library's materials, as well as other types of shelving designed for newspapers, records, or magazines. The study areas may have tables and carrels suitable for studying or writing. Special study areas may be furnished also with sofas and easy chairs for your use.

Some libraries set aside study rooms that you may be able to reserve for a few hours if you feel that you could benefit from a private area or if you are working with a group of people and do not wish to disturb others. While you are becoming familiar with these areas, become familiar with the library's policies on noise, food and drink, and smoking. Special rooms may be designated for refreshments, smoking, or social conversations. Since you may be spending some time in the library working on your research paper, it is a good idea to figure out how you can maximize your comfort at the same time.

The Search Strategy

Sooner or later, however, all of these preliminary activities must end, and you will have to actually begin work to find materials for your research paper. Now the big question to consider is the starting point: in the mass of material available to you in a college library, where do you actually begin your search for relevant information?

Even in libraries that contain a million or more books, there is a logical starting point for every information search. Many librarians use the term *search strategy* for this process of deciding what to look at first, then second, and so on. Usually, it is best to try to look at general information resources first; then move on to material that contains specific information. By the time you get to the specific information resources, you should have decided on a definite form of your research topic, and you will not waste time reading information that is not relevant to your paper. If you follow a good plan in your collection of research material, you will be able to reach the end of your research effort with the comforting thought that you have found most of the material relevant to your topic and available in your library.

Basic Steps in a Search Strategy

Good research plans, or search strategies, usually contain four basic steps:

1. Start with sources of **introductory information,** especially if you are unfamiliar with your topic. Such sources include encyclopedias, dictionaries, almanacs, yearbooks, and guides to the literature on a certain subject. Encyclopedias and dictionaries may be general in nature (such as the *Encyclopedia Americana* and *The Merriam-Webster Dictionary*), or they may be focused on one subject area (such as *The Encyclopedia of Philosophy* and *The Dictionary of Genetics*). Although you would probably not want to use information taken from these sources directly in your research paper, they do provide a background for your research effort. Usually these introductory information sources are found in the reference area of your library.

2. Next, move to sources of **comprehensive information,** which normally means information contained in books or government documents. Since you now have a general idea of what your topic is about, you can try to find whole books and government documents that deal with the topic. Comprehensive information sources may be found in various storage areas throughout your library. You will identify the available materials and their locations by using the library's catalog (which will be discussed in detail, later in this chapter).

3. After you have assembled a group of books on your topic, the next logical step is to look for **specific information** that would

be contained in physical units smaller than an entire book. These physical units may be magazine or newspaper articles, or they may be chapters in other books. You learn about the existence of this material by using different indexes (a process that will be examined later).

4. Finally, you can attempt to evaluate the material you have collected by looking at sources of **evaluative information.** This process usually means looking for reviews of the books you have located to determine if the book's author and its information were regarded as authoritative and accurate at the time the book was published. You might want to know this information before you base your entire paper on the opinions of one author.

Before we begin a detailed discussion of these four steps, we would like to summarize them in a brief example. If you were actually working on the topic of how the Federal Reserve Bank attempts to control inflation, you might want to begin by reading an encyclopedia article on the Federal Reserve system. Next you could find several books on the Federal Reserve system, and perhaps some documents published by the United States Government about this agency. Once you have examined this material, you would be ready to look for specific articles in newspapers or magazines about efforts by the Federal Reserve Bank to control inflation. Finally, you could attempt to evaluate this information by using various reviews of the authors and books you have located.

Now, we are ready to look in detail at exactly how you find relevant material in your library. This discussion will be presented using the four-part search strategy outline described earlier, and will also mention some reference sources commonly found in college libraries. It will also assume that you are already familiar with the physical layout of your library.

Step 1: Introductory Information

Introductory information is best located by asking a member of the library staff at the reference or information desk for directions to the reference area. Usually the encyclopedias and dictionaries are kept in a separate reference area, and it is easy to browse through this reference area once you find it. Most of the information sources in the reference area will not be difficult to use. Your library experiences in high school should have taught you how an encyclopedia is organized, with a basically alphabetical arrangement of articles supplemented by a detailed index of names, places, and subjects. Some of the information sources in the reference area may not be entirely self-explanatory, however, and in these cases you should first look in the front pages of the book to see if it has a section that explains how to use the book. If it does not, or if the explanation is complex, then take the book to the reference desk and ask a library staff member for assistance. You can also ask the library staff to help you find introductory material on a certain topic.

Step 2: Comprehensive Information

Comprehensive information is usually located by using the library's catalog. A few years ago this item would have been referred to as the card catalog, but that term is disappearing as new forms of the catalog appear. Although the card format is still the most common, you may find library catalogs in various formats, such as microfiche or microfilm, as well as on computer terminals. Regardless of the form, the basic purpose of the library catalog is to tell you which books are available. You can use any one of three access points to ask this question. For example, the catalog will tell you how many books by a certain **author** are located in your library. It will also tell you how many books with a certain **title** your library owns. Finally, you can discover how many books on a certain **subject** your library has. (The approach by subject will probably be the most useful access point for your research project.)

Although your library may not have a card catalog, whatever catalog format it has will present information about books in card images similar to the one shown in Exhibit 2.1. This card contains a great deal of valuable information about a certain book, and it would prove helpful if you could learn how to interpret the various codes and symbols used by your library. A typical card in the author area of the catalog is pictured as Exhibit 2.1. This is a catalog card for the book entitled *Organization Theory* which was written by William G. Scott. The information included on this catalog card is separated into several groups, which have been numbered in the illustration and are discussed next. If you read all of the elements of a catalog card, you can learn much information about a book before you decide to look for it on the library shelves. This card was chosen for this example because its style is typical of cards now being used in many college libraries. Your library may use a different format, but the information presented should be essentially the same. If you have difficulty interpreting any part of a catalog card, remember to ask a library staff member at the reference desk for assistance.

The numbers in Exhibit 2.1 refer to the following elements of information.

1. **Call Number:** The book will be placed on the library shelves in accordance with this combination of letters and numbers. Several

EXHIBIT 2.1   Author, title, and subject cards for the same book.

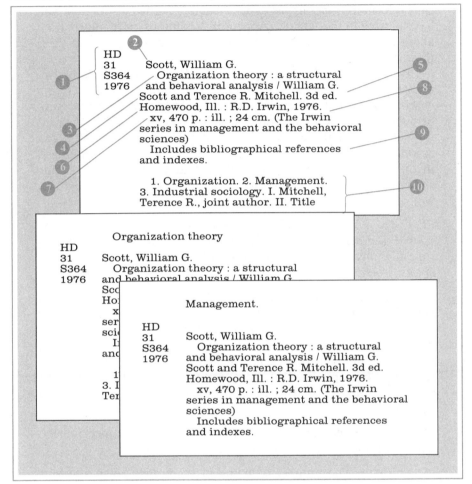

different call number plans are used by college libraries. The most frequent are the Library of Congress classification, the Dewey Decimal classification, and the Superintendent of Documents classification. The first two classification systems are generally used for book collections, while the Superintendent of Documents classification system is used for collections for documents of the federal government.

For a librarian, each line of a call number has a specific meaning related to the book's subject, title, author, or date of publication. At this point in your library work, you do not necessarily need to understand the complete significance of each line of the call number. However, the first line of the call number does contain significant information about the general subject matter of the item you have located in the catalog. (Appendix A contains more information about the significance of the first line of the call numbers in these three classifications.)

It is important that you know where books with this call number would be shelved in your library. You should be able to find a chart or guide that will explain where books with certain call numbers are located. After all, your ultimate reason for locating the card for the book in the catalog is to find the actual book. You can accomplish this by understanding the location symbols contained in the call number. Before you try to find a certain book on the shelves, be sure you have written down the entire call number. You will need all of it to find the exact book you need for your paper.

2. Entry: This is usually the name of the main author of the book. For other books, this space may contain the name of a responsible organization or just the book title, if the book has no main author.

3. Title: The book's title, along with any subtitles, are presented here. For example, the title of this book is *Organization Theory*. The subtitle is *A Structural and Behavioral Analysis*. Don't be disturbed if the catalog card does not capitalize certain words in the title which you feel should be capitalized (or which your documentation guide says *must* be capitalized). Library capitalization rules are not the standard capitalization rules most people use, so you are not bound by them.

4. Author: The name of the book's main author is repeated here, along with the names of any joint authors.

5. Edition: The number or name of the edition of the book is given here. For example, this is a card for the third edition of the book, which means that two previous editions have already been published. The information in the book represents an attempt by the authors to update what was presented earlier. The later editions are helpful if you are looking for the most current material on your subject.

6. Imprint: This is a library term that refers to the area containing publishing information about the book. It usually includes the place of publication, the name of the publisher, and the date of publication. You should write down this information for later use in your notes and bibliography.

7. Collation: This library term refers to the area containing information about the number of pages, presence of illustrations, and the

size of the book. This particular book was 470 pages (and 15 pages in front matter). You might want to know the length if you are looking for a short book to read on your topic. The presence or absence of illustrations might also influence your choice of a book to use for your project.

8. Series: Some books are published as members of a group of books on a certain subject. This group of books will have a group title; in this case, it is *The Irwin Series in Management and the Behavioral Sciences.* Usually, this information is of interest to you only if you are trying to find the other books in this set or series.

9. Notes: This area contains other miscellaneous information. The note on this card means that the book, in addition to its text, contains a list of references on the book's subject and an index. If you are still collecting research sources for your working bibliography, you might want to use the list of references in this book to add a few titles you may not have found already.

10. Tracings: This is another library term. The *tracings* are the access points for the other cards in your catalog for this book. Every access point, as will be discussed later, is represented in the catalog by a card such as this. So you can find a card for this book regardless of whether you looked up the subjects of *organization, management,* or *industrial sociology.* You could also have looked up the name of the joint author, Mitchell, Terence R. instead of Scott, William G.

Access Points

Let's discuss the issue of access points a little more. You can locate books in the catalog by author, title, and subject. In some libraries the catalogs for these various access points are physically separated. For example, if you wanted to look up a certain book by its author, you would go to the author catalog. Cards arranged by subject would be found in the subject catalog. Other libraries have all cards for all access points filed in one catalog. If you have difficulty with this catalog format, you should ask a library staff member for assistance before proceeding further.

Since you will probably be using the subject access point primarily, let us examine this issue in greater detail. If you wish to find books on a certain subject, you would look in the subject catalog (if your library has a separate catalog for this access point) for books on your subject. The catalog cards in this catalog will be arranged alphabetically by subjects. If you were looking for a book on management, for example, you would first look for the section in the subject catalog that has cards starting with the word *Management.* Since your library probably has many books on this topic, there will be many cards with this same access point heading. In most libraries, access points with many books are subdivided into smaller groups for your convenience. Thus, you may find in addition to *Management* the subtopics of *Management-History* and *Management-Study and Teaching.* By this method, the subject catalog will assist you in finding books on specific areas within the overall subject of management.

Subjects may be individual words, such *Geology* or *Paradox.* They may be word combinations, such as *Department stores* or *Aesthetics, medieval.* They may also be phrases, such as *Indians of North America* or *Television broadcasting of news.* Subjects may be names of places, such as *China* or *Yazoo City, Mississippi.* They may also be personal names, such as *Descartes, Réné, 1596–1650* or *Faulkner, William, 1897–1962.*

The standard form of these subject terms has always been a problem for library users. In the example given, *Aesthetics, medieval* is a standard subject term; *Medieval aesthetics* would not be such a term. Although information can be published on an infinite number of subjects or combinations of subjects, libraries have traditionally not used an infinitely large group of subject terms to classify this information. Usually, a library will use a standard list of subject terms. The standard list may contain several hundred thousand terms, and two or three of these terms will adequately describe the subject content of a particular publication. One such standard subject list that many libraries use is the *Library of Congress Subject Headings.* This index is usually available near the catalog. If you consult it, you can not only see which subject headings are actually used by your library, you can also determine the exact form and spelling of the headings.

Alphabetical Arrangement

It is difficult to generalize about the arrangement of the cards in the catalog of your library. The arrangement is usually alphabetical; but as you might imagine, the alphabetical rules for filing a million or more cards, some of which start with access points such as *Hall-Edward, Timothy* and *101 nights in a barroom,* can become quite complicated. *101 nights in a barroom* could logically be filed in any of the following sequences.

1. In a section of the catalog arranged numerically:

> 40 cats sat on my hat
> 101 nights in a barroom
> 200 famous Black Americans

2. In a section of the catalog arranged alphabetically with numerals spelled out as words:

One life to live
101 nights in a barroom (i.e., One zero one nights . . .)
One zesty dessert

3. In a section of the catalog arranged alphabetically with numerals spelled out as they would be pronounced:

One elephant came to dinner
101 nights in a barroom (i.e., One hundred and one nights . . .)
1000 Mexican folk tales (i.e., One thousand Mexican . . .)
One yucca tree remains

Most college libraries will file *101 nights in a barroom* according to the third example. If you have difficulty finding a certain card or area of the catalog, ask a member of the library staff for help. The staff may also have a guide that you can consult to learn the particular alphabetical rules used by your library.

Comprehensive Information: Government Documents

We mentioned earlier that in addition to using the library catalog to find comprehensive material in books, you might also want to locate similar material in government documents. Most college libraries receive books, pamphlets, and technical reports published by the various agencies of the United States Government. Such publications are usually referred to as *government documents.* Some college libraries also have sections for state and local government publications.

Documents can be a very valuable source of information, particularly if you are doing a research paper on any issue involving public policy, social issues, or economic matters. To locate federal government documents, you will probably use a catalog published by the U.S. Government. This catalog, called the *Monthly Catalog of United States Government Publications,* is actually a book with pages filled with images of catalog cards. (Such catalogs are often called book catalogs, for obvious reasons.) The catalog description for one item in a recent volume is presented as Exhibit 2.2.

This example represents an annual report by the government agency responsible for managing our strategic petroleum reserve program, which is an effort to store a large amount of petroleum to be used in the event of another oil embargo. The catalog entry contains much information about the report and about various call numbers libraries can use for this item. You should consult a member of the library staff for assistance in locating and interpreting gov-

EXHIBIT 2.2   A portion of the *Monthly Catalog of United States Government Publications.*

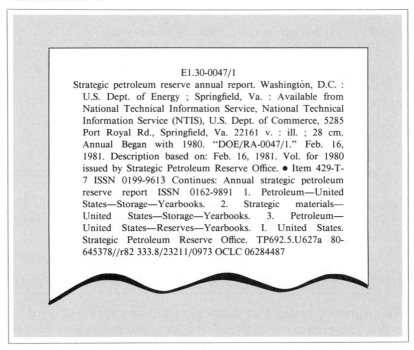

E1.30-0047/1
Strategic petroleum reserve annual report. Washington, D.C. : U.S. Dept. of Energy ; Springfield, Va. : Available from National Technical Information Service, National Technical Information Service (NTIS), U.S. Dept. of Commerce, 5285 Port Royal Rd., Springfield, Va. 22161 v. : ill. ; 28 cm. Annual Began with 1980. "DOE/RA-0047/1." Feb. 16, 1981. Description based on: Feb. 16, 1981. Vol. for 1980 issued by Strategic Petroleum Reserve Office. ● Item 429-T-7 ISSN 0199-9613 Continues: Annual strategic petroleum reserve report ISSN 0162-9891 1. Petroleum—United States—Storage—Yearbooks. 2. Strategic materials—United States—Storage—Yearbooks. 3. Petroleum—United States—Reserves—Yearbooks. I. United States. Strategic Petroleum Reserve Office. TP692.5.U627a 80-645378//r82 333.8/23211/0973 OCLC 06284487

ernment documents such as this. In large college libraries there may be a special department that is responsible for documents, and you can ask for guidance there.

Specific Information: Book Chapters

One additional source of specific information that you may want to use provides access to book chapter material. As you have just learned, you can find whole books on a certain topic by looking in the subject area of your library catalog. However, it is true that each year many books are published that contain a variety of specific chapters, all of which are probably about the same general topic but which cannot be found using the library's subject catalog. For example, a book on world economics in the twentieth century may contain fifteen chapters, each on the economy of a specific country. The library cannot place a card in the catalog for each of these individual topics (such as *Economy-France* and *Economy-Egypt*). Instead, there would be one subject card, which would simply be some general economic subject heading. If you were really interested in the economy of Egypt, you would not be able to locate this particular chapter of the book using the library catalog. However, you could use the *Essay and General Literature Index,* which is an index to book chapter material. A portion of a page from this index is reproduced as Exhibit 2.3.

As you can see from this example, if you were interested in American economic assistance, you could find a chapter on such assistance to Norway. This chapter was written by E. Erichsen, and is entitled "Norway: twenty years after the Marshall Plan." It may be found on pages 163–177 of the book entitled *Inflation, Trade, and Taxes.* If you wish to read this chapter, your next step will be to determine whether or not this book is in your library. To accomplish this, you will have to go to the catalog and look for this title. If the book is in your library, you should find a card for it filed by the title. Then, you would jot down the call number and look for the book at the appropriate place on the shelves.

Specific Information: Magazines

Once you have located a variety of comprehensive material in book or document form, you should be ready to begin looking for specific

EXHIBIT 2.3   A portion of a page from the *Essay and General Literature Index.*

Economic assistance, American
    Bickerton, I. J. Foreign aid. *In* Encyclopedia of American foreign policy p372-79
    Smith, G. The Marshall plan. *In* Encyclopedia of American foreign policy p535-44

Norway
    Erichsen, E. Norway: twenty years after the Marshall plan. *In* Inflation, trade and taxes p163-77

information in magazines, newspapers, or in book chapters. In order to do this efficiently, you must become familiar with indexes to the material. If you need a magazine article on *Georgia,* you do not begin the search by sitting down with a set of *National Geographic* magazines and thumbing through the pages until you come across an article on the subject. As you might imagine, this strategy is not the easiest way to accomplish the task. There are many publishers who prepare indexes to certain types of magazines. By using one or more of these indexes, you can determine where and when magazine articles on your subject have been published. Then you can begin finding those magazine articles in your library.

The Reader's Guide to Periodical Literature

One basic magazine index is the *Reader's Guide to Periodical Literature.* It is found in almost all college libraries, although these libraries will also have more sophisticated indexes that you will want to use later. These indexes contain detailed indexing information for magazines related to a certain subject, such as art, biology, or sociology. The *Reader's Guide* indexes almost 200 magazines on many subjects of general interest. A portion of a page from the Reader's Guide is presented as Exhibit 2.4.

If you were looking for magazine articles on Georgia (and did not want to flip through magazines at random), this section of this particular index would direct you to several articles on the subject. Depending on the particular focus of your research, you could choose from articles about Georgia's antiquities, its legislature, its parks and reserves, and so on. Each of the entries in this index is called a *citation* and gives you the information about the article that you will need in order to find it on the shelves of your library. In Exhibit 2.4, one citation has been highlighted for closer examination.

This citation, which begins "Governor vs. governor," tells you that an article with this title was written by S. Chapman and was published in the *Atlantic* magazine in October 1980. The issue with this date was part of Volume 246 of this magazine, and the article begins on page 6 of the issue. You can also learn that the article contains illustrations (the *il* abbreviation) and that the article continues on later pages of the same issue (the + sign).

Once you have assembled several interesting citations, you will next need to determine whether or not your library has the magazines and the particular issues specified in the citations. You must realize that indexes often include magazine titles that are not available in all libraries. Obviously, larger libraries have more of these

EXHIBIT 2.4   A portion of a page from the *Reader's Guide to Periodical Literature.*

GEORGIA
  See also
  Architecture, Domestic—Georgia ·
  Chickamauga and Chattanooga National Military
    Park
  Child welfare—Georgia
  Criminal justice. Administration of—Georgia
  Cumberland Island National Seashore
  Education—Georgia
  Festivals—Georgia
  Libraries—Georgia
  Music festivals—Georgia
  Opera—Georgia
  Restaurants—Georgia
  Trials—Georgia
          Antiquities
  North Georgia's mysterious mounds (Etowah
    Indian Mounds) il South Liv 15:50 My '80
          Legislature
  Creationist bill dies in Georgia legislature. K
    S. Saladin. Humanist 40:59–60 My/Je '80
  Georgia legislators rest before creating bill
    (proposal mandating teaching of creation
    whenever evolution is taught) A. H. Matthews.
    Chr Today 24:51 Ap 18 '80
  Science, religion and the Georgia legislature (bill
    mandating teaching of scientific creationism)
    B. Jones. Chr Cent 98:6–8 Ja 7–14 '81
          Parks and reserves
  Canyon cut through clay (Providence Canyon
    State Park) il map South Liv 15:54 D '80
  Stone Mountain State Park. R. Magruder and
    M. Magruder. il Trav/Holiday 153:78-9+ My
    '80
          Politics and government
      See also
  Georgia—Legislature
  Primaries—Georgia

  Governor vs. governor: Reagan's and Carter's
    performances. S. Chapman. il Atlantic 246:6+
    O '80

titles, and smaller libraries fewer of them. Even if your library has a certain magazine, it may not have all volumes or issues.

For example, if you are interested in a magazine article published in *Time* in 1952, your library may have begun its subscription to *Time* in 1953. So although the magazine is available, the particular issue is not. Your library should have a guide to its periodicals collection that you can use to determine which volumes of which magazines are actually available in your library. The list may be in the form of another card file, computer printout, or microform. It is important that you become familiar with this guide before you begin your work with magazine and journal indexes, so that you know whether or not the material you locate in the indexes will be available in your library.

You will also have to become familiar with the location of the magazines in your library. Some libraries maintain old copies of magazines in their original form, although the volumes may have been strengthened by binding them with cloth and cardboard covers. Other libraries replace their paper copies of magazines with copies in microformats. Microforms are miniaturized copies of the original material on long strips of photographic film (microfilm) or on flat photographic film cards (microfiche). You should realize that microform is not a type of recorded information, such as books, magazines, or newspapers. It is merely a way to store information. In the past, almost all recorded information was stored in a paper format. Now we can store this same information in microforms or, in some cases, directly in a computerized data system.

If your library does have magazines available on microfilm or on microfiche, you will need to ask a library staff member for information on locating and using this type of material. You might also want to allow yourself extra time when using microforms. Instead of simply flipping to the desired page in a paper volume, you will have to mount a microform volume in a reading machine and advance the film or fiche until you reach the correct location.

Specific Information: Newspapers

With the exception of the most current issues, newspapers are almost always available in libraries in a microform format. In order to find an article on a certain subject, you use a newspaper index, much as you would use a magazine index. A portion of a page from the 1981 index to the *New York Times* is shown in as Exhibit 2.5.

One article in the *Geology* section is highlighted. Instead of a title, you are given a summary of the article's content. This article

EXHIBIT 2.5   A portion of a page from the 1981 index to the *New York Times.*

> GEOLOGY. See also specific subjects, eg, Earthquakes, Oceans, Volcanoes
>
> Follow-up on hydrogen maser, used to measure time from energy emitted by stimulated hydrogen atoms; maser was developed by Johns Hopkins University Applied Physics Laboratory; NASA Crustal Dynamics Project manager Dr Robert Coates says group is using 8 clocks to measure movements in earth's crust (S), Ja 18.33:1
>
> Christopher Lehmann-Haupt reviews John McPhee book Basin and Range; illustration. My 8.III.27:1; Paul Zweig reviews book; illustrations. My 17.VII.p1
>
> Article on scientific studies of earth tides that scientists hope can resolve questions about elasticity of earth's internal layers, churning and rotation of molten material in core and possible role of tidal motions in triggering earthquakes and in causing wobbles in earth's spin (M), Ag 23.56.1
>
> Calif Univ geographers find evidence of biological genesis of manganese-rich desert varnishes that leave coating on desert rocks (S). S 15.III.2:2
>
> USSR announces expansion of continental drilling program calling for some 20 holes up to 7 miles deep (M), S 29.III. 3:1
>
> Space shuttle Columbia's cargo bay will carry scientific experiments, including mapping radar and infrared scanning system to identify geologic formation of econ interest; drawing (M), N 4.23:1

concerns the use of the shuttle program to assist in geologic exploration. It appeared on page 23, column 1, of the November 4, 1981 issue of the paper. You can also learn that the article contains at least one drawing and is about two columns long (the *M* is an abbreviation for medium length).

Evaluative Information: Book Reviews

One final step in locating relevant material is to obtain information that evaluates the sources you have chosen for your paper, which is fairly easy to do for books. The *Book Review Digest* is one of several indexes that gives you access to reviews of books. A portion of a page from this index is reproduced as Exhibit 2.6.

The highlighted entry represents reviews of the book by Terry

EXHIBIT 2.6   A portion of a page from the *Book Review Digest.*

SANFORD, TERRY. A danger of democracy; the Presidential nominating process. 154p $12.95 1981 Westview Press

324.5 Presidents—United States—Nomination

ISBN 0-86531-159-5   LC 80-29535

The author, "former North Carolina governor and current president of Duke University feels the presidential nominating process is 'fraught with danger and uncertainty.' The purpose of his ... series of essays is 'to lift lessons from the fascinating history of party nominations.... . to suggest some conclusions about present inadequacies,' and to propose a new philosophy for the nominating process that is at once democratic, republican, traditional and radical. Sanford argues for a more deliberative nominating process and for more 'thinking delegates' at the party conventions." (Library J) Bibliography. Index.

"Sanford—despite his easy prose and open style —is, in fact, quite deeply troubled about the way in which we select our most important political leader. His altogether logical underlying assumption: a faulty selection process will inevitably mean a much-weaker-than-necessary chief executive. The early part of this slim volume is history, tales—with a hint of nostalgia—of presidential selections from our distant and more recent past.... Presidential scholars will be familiar with the main themes of this book. Moreover, academics have reached virtual consensus on items such as the decline of the party, and how lamentable that is: the chaos of the current primary system, and how lamentable that is. Sanford's book, though, has two special strengths: its accessibility to those who are not so familiar with the ground it covers, and the sense of urgency it conveys about a defect in our political machinery." Barbara Kellerman

Ann Am Acad 461:1S1 My '82 600w

"Sanford clearly fears that our current system of nominating presidents has become unrepresentative in our attempts to make it more 'democratic.' The very compact book is loaded with too many folksy and anecdotal passages. Someone once remarked that good political scientists do not make great governors. Likewise, good governors do not necessarily make great political scientists."

Choice 19:308 O '81 310w

"[This] well-crafted book raises fundamental questions about presidential selection and clarifies the role and responsibilities political parties should reclaim." E. C. Dreyer

Library J 106:1429 Jl '81 130w

Sanford, entitled *A Danger of Democracy,* which was published in 1981 by Westview Press. You are presented with a summary of the book's themes and then with excerpts from reviews in three different magazines. The middle review (beginning with "Sanford clearly fears . . .") informs you that although this book may be a worthwhile contribution to American political commentary, it is not a serious work by a respected political scientist. You might want to know this information before you incorporate Sanford's opinions into your research paper.

Summary

We have discussed locating library material for your research paper by following a search strategy, which should lead you from general, introductory information to highly specific information directly pertinent to your topic. Throughout the discussion we have emphasized the fact that your familiarity with the physical layout and the services provided by your college library will enhance your ability to actually locate the material you need. Every library is unique in its arrangement of material. You can make your research effort easier by becoming familiar with the library before you begin serious work, by formulating and following a logical search strategy, and by fully utilizing the assistance offered by the staff of your library during your work.

CHAPTER 3

USING THE LIBRARY— WHAT AND WHERE

All searches for information have a beginning. However, few reach a definite ending. It is a rare occasion when a researcher can feel secure that all of the information on a topic has been found. Instead, the researcher usually follows a trail of information from one resource to another, until enough material has been located to satisfy the purposes of the research project.

Your college library staff usually will not help you decide where to end your particular search. Such a decision, which depends on the topic, the intent, and the depth of the research, is usually a matter between the researcher and his or her colleagues or instructors. Your library staff is better organized to help you begin your research and to aid you with its progress along the way.

This chapter lists several information resources that you might want to consider when beginning your search for information. Most of the particular titles listed in the following sections are commonly found in even the smallest college libraries. Of course, larger libraries will have many additional resources that will help you get started in your work.

The following resources are listed by type in an order that approximates the search strategy outline described in Chapter 2—Introductory, Comprehensive, Specific, and Evaluative. If you wish to use any of these resources, of course, you will first have to determine their location in your library by consulting your library's catalog or by asking a staff member. Since new volumes or editions of many of these items are published each year, the date of publication is not included in the listings provided here. Your library's catalog will show you the latest edition of each resource.

Dictionaries

Dictionaries exist in general and subject forms. Such general dictionaries would include *Webster's Third,* the *Oxford English Dictionary,* and *Webster's New Collegiate.* The *Oxford English Dictionary* also contains information that will help you trace historical changes in the use of a certain word. Subject dictionaries, such as the *Dictionary of Genetics* and the *Handbook to Literature,* exist for almost every topic. These dictionaries often contain a short discussion of a term, in addition to its definition.

1. *Webster's Third New International Dictionary of the English Language, Unabridged.* Springfield, Massachusetts: G. & C. Merriam Company.

2. *The Oxford English Dictionary.* Oxford: Clarendon Press.

3. *Webster's New Collegiate Dictionary.* Springfield, Massachusetts: G. & C. Merriam Company.

4. King, Robert C. *A Dictionary of Genetics.* New York: Oxford University Press.

5. Holman, C. Hugh. *An Handbook to Literature.* Indianapolis: The Odyssey Press.

Encyclopedias

The *Encyclopedia Americana* and the *Encyclopaedia Britannica* are two examples of general encyclopedias. Usually published in multiple volumes, a general encyclopedia attempts to contain at least some information on virtually any topic. Of course, the depth of this information is necessarily limited. Although you probably will not want to use encyclopedia information as a major resource material for your project, you can use general encyclopedias for a quick introduction to a subject, to verify certain facts, and to see how a discussion of your subject could be organized.

In addition to general encyclopedias, there are also many subject encyclopedias that contain information on topics related to one broad subject area. If you were working with a research project on Greek philosophers, you would find more information on Plato in the *Encyclopedia of Philosophy* than would appear in the *Encyclopedia Americana.*

1. *The Encyclopedia Americana.* Danbury, Connecticut: Americana Corporation.

2. *The New Encyclopaedia Britannica.* Chicago: Encyclopaedia Britannica, Inc.

3. *The Encyclopedia of Philosophy.* New York: The Macmillan Company & The Free Press.

4. *New Catholic Encyclopedia.* New York: McGraw-Hill Book Company.

5. *McGraw-Hill Encyclopedia of Science & Technology.* New York: McGraw-Hill Book Company.

6. *The Encyclopedia of Education.* New York: The Macmillan Company & The Free Press.

Almanacs

An almanac is a book of facts and figures often arranged in tables, charts, or lists for quick reference. The *Statistical Abstract* is the best introductory source for factual information about the population, the economy, or the society of the United States. It will also refer you to more comprehensive information in the publications of the United States Government.

1. *The World Almanac and Book of Facts.* New York: Newspaper Enterprise Association, Inc.

2. *Statistical Abstract of the United States.* Washington, D.C.: Government Printing Office.

Catalogs of Books

Your library will have a list of books that are available in its collection. This list may appear in any of the following formats: (1) on 3-x-5 cards; (2) in printed books; (3) on rolls of microfilm; (4) on sheets of microfiche; (5) on computer terminals. Some libraries have only one copy of their catalog, and this copy (usually a card catalog) is located at a central point in the library itself. Other libraries have many copies of their catalog (usually in a microformat) available throughout the library and other college buildings.

Many college libraries list their books by subject according to the subject terms that appear in the *Library of Congress Subject Headings.* This resource will help you decide which subject terms are appropriate for your search. It will also suggest terms for additional subjects that are related to your main topic.

Publications of the United States Government and all of its various agencies are listed in the *Monthly Catalog of the United States Government Publications,* which is an example of a catalog in book form.

The *Essay and General Literature Index* serves as a guide to chapter-length material on specific subjects that may have been published in books with a more general overall topic.

A bibliography is a list of books. In a sense, your library catalog is a giant bibliography. If you need information on butterflies, you look up *butterflies* in your library's catalog. However, this catalog is limited to book-type material. The *Bibliographic Index* does not have this limitation. It contains subject lists of books, magazine articles, and other types of publications that contain bibliographies themselves. If you looked up *butterflies,* you may find four books and three magazine articles. Each of these seven items contains a list of other publications about butterflies. This list is a quick way to assemble a long bibliography on a given topic.

1. Your library's catalog.

2. *Library of Congress Subject Headings.* Washington, D.C.: The Library of Congress.

3. *Monthly Catalog of United States Government Publications.* Washington, D.C.: Government Printing Office.

4. *Essay and General Literature Index.* New York: The H. W. Wilson Company.

5. *Bibliographic Index.* New York: The H. W. Wilson Company.

Biography

Several resources we have listed, such as the general encyclopedias, will also contain biographical material. However, specialized biographical resources, such as the *Current Biography Yearbook* and the *Encyclopedia of World Biography,* are also available. *Biography Index* does not have actual biographical data, but instead provides an index that will lead you to such information published elsewhere. For example, if a magazine article on a certain company contained a biographical sketch of the company's founder, an entry for that article would be included in *Biography Index.*

1. *Current Biography Yearbook.* New York: The H. W. Wilson Company.

2. *The McGraw-Hill Encyclopedia of World Biography.* New York: McGraw-Hill Book Company.

3. *Biography Index.* New York: The H. W. Wilson Company.

Magazine Indexes

The *Reader's Guide to Periodical Literature* is the standard general magazine index. Including almost 200 magazine titles, *Reader's Guide* will help you locate major articles by the access points of subject or author. However, *Reader's Guide* will not contain extensive indexing for any one subject, and probably should not be relied upon exclusively for college-level research projects.

To supplement the general magazine indexes such as *Reader's Guide,* there are hundreds of subject indexes that concentrate on journals in a specific subject area. The indexes listed below are examples of such subject indexes. They are produced by the same publishing company, so they share a similar organization and index-ing style. When you learn to use one, you will find the others easy to use.

1. *Reader's Guide to Periodical Literature.* New York: The H. W. Wilson Company.

2. *Education Index.* New York: The H. W. Wilson Company.

3. *General Science Index.* New York: The H. W. Wilson Company.

4. *Business Periodicals Index.* New York: The H. W. Wilson Company.

5. *Humanities Index.* New York: The H. W. Wilson Company.

6. *Art Index.* New York: The H. W. Wilson Company.

Newspaper Indexes

Although your library will probably have some current newspapers in paper form, older issues will often be kept in microformat. You can get access to information in the older newspapers by using a newspaper index such as the two listed below. Indexes are usually available for newspapers of national importance. A member of your library staff can tell you if your library has indexes for other regional or local newspapers.

1. *The New York Times Index.* New York: The New York Times Company.

2. *The Wall Street Journal Index.* New York: Dow Jones & Company, Inc.

Evaluative Information

Not only best-sellers are reviewed; almost every book published in the United States is reviewed by one publication or another. You can use the following indexes to locate such reviews, and the reviews will help you evaluate the merit of the book itself. In addi-tion to giving you the source of the review, the *Book Review Digest* also provides excerpts from the text of the reviews themselves.

1. *Current Book Review Citations.* New York: The H. W. Wilson Company.

2. *Book Review Index.* Detroit: Gale Research Company.

3. *Book Review Digest.* New York: The H. W. Wilson Company.

1. Compare two encyclopedia entries on a famous event, a natural disaster, a battle in a war, a national election or a public figure and note any differences, even small ones, between the two.

2. Find an article on a controversial subject in the *Reader's Guide to Periodical Literature* and list the words or phrases that indicate the bias of the article.

3. Use your library's catalog to locate a book on the subject of automobiles.

4. Photocopy an article from a journal in your major and list the information in it that might lead you to additional material relating to the topic of the article (names, places, dates, for example).

5. Find a biography or autobiography of some famous person and then look for reviews of this book in the *Book Review Digest*. How was the book received by reviewers?

CHAPTER 4

COMPILING A
BIBLIOGRAPHY

Methods of taking notes differ. Some people prefer 3-x-5 cards; others, 4-x-6. Some like notebook paper, while others insist on typing all notes. Still others, familiar with state-of-the-art technology, transfer notes into the storage devices of portable microcomputers.

Some researchers use note cards for more than quotations or summaries from sources. In some instances, researchers include comments about the tone of the material; brief biographical comments about the author, which might prove to be useful when composing the paper; or references to other sources, which might make organization easier. When a researcher elects to add such information, larger note cards (5-x-8) may prove to be more useful.

As you begin collecting information and taking notes, make sure that you have a system for storing cards, outlines, and drafts— possibly a large envelope or a small waterproof box. With a small file box, you can separate and order material from several different sources.

The following method of taking notes has proved successful over many years. It is not the only way to ensure accuracy and coherence, but it is especially helpful to beginners. After you have mastered this method, you may indeed see ways to modify it to better suit your needs in various disciplines and to adapt to technological advances in word processing.

Step 1: Compiling Bibliographical Data

When you are ready to take your first note, write the complete bibliographical entry for your source, exactly as it will appear in the final draft, on the back of a notecard. (See Exhibit 4.1.) For note cards from the same source, label the back of each card with the author's last name only. Number each card from the same source consecutively. When you change authors, change cards and again give complete bibliographical data, starting over with number 1. (See Exhibit 4.2.)

If you have more than one book or article by the same author, or if you have two or more sources by authors with the same last names, use short titles and first names to distinguish them from each other, on subsequent notecards. Exhibits 4.3, 4.4, and 4.5 illustrate the three different types of entries. Remember: when you change sources, give complete bibliographical data and start over with your numbering.

EXHIBIT 4.1   The first card: complete bibliographical entry written on the back of the card.

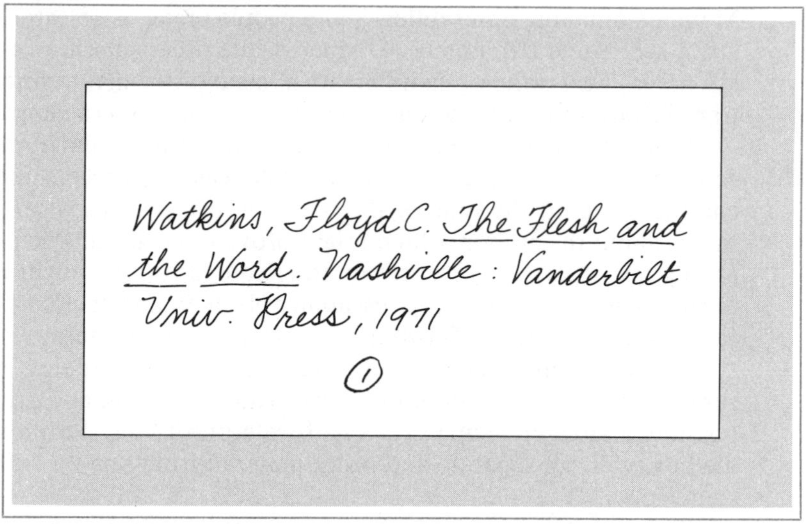

EXHIBIT 4.2   A note card, numbered consecutively. This exhibit shows the back of card 2.

EXHIBIT 4.3 Two cards showing the same author for different sources, written on back of card.

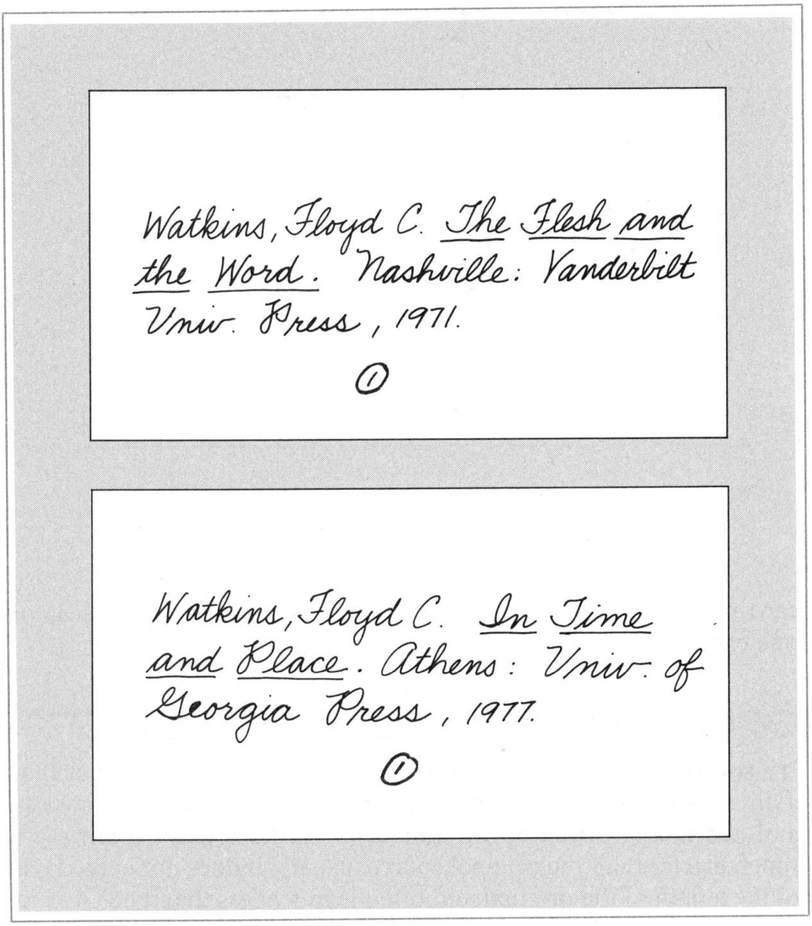

Watkins, Floyd C. *The Flesh and the Word*. Nashville: Vanderbilt Univ. Press, 1971.

①

Watkins, Floyd C. *In Time and Place*. Athens: Univ. of Georgia Press, 1977.

①

Step 2: Paginating Sources

After you have carefully given the complete bibliographical entry on the back of your card, you are ready to write your first note on the front of the card. The first and very important step in this process is to give the page number of the information. You will need all page numbers to document your sources; be accurate here and write the page number before any other information. If you take information from more than one page, then be sure to show all changes in pagination on your note card. Begin this process of notetaking on the second line of your card; do not write on the first line (the red one) at the top of the card. (See Exhibit 4.6.) Taking only one note per

EXHIBIT 4.4   A subsequent card with a short title to distinguish works by the same author, also on the back of a card.

card may help you avoid possible confusion with several ideas on one card.

Step 3: Summarizing, Paraphrasing, and Quoting

If a source is very long, you should consider a summary rather than a direct quotation. To summarize well, take the essence of a passage and put this information in your own words. A good summary is much briefer than the original source; usually it does not exceed half of the length of the original and often is much less than half. A paraphrase, on the other hand, is about the same length as the original, but in your own words. It is useful for explanation of complex passages. The following passage is directly quoted from an article by Carey Lovelace entitled "Painting for Dollars" which appeared in the July, 1983, issue of *Harper's*. A summary of the original passage follows the direct quotation.

Direct quotation:

> A new generation of American artists has rejected the modernist notion of art as a "spiritual project" (in the words of Susan Sontag). Abandoning the elitist alienation that was the hallmark of their predecessors, they have thrown themselves wholeheartedly into the art market, a world increasingly embracing salesmanship and public relations. They are now consciously trying to create works that people will both enjoy and buy.

EXHIBIT 4.5 Cards (a) and (b) illustrate cards for different authors with the same surname. Card (c) is the back of a subsequent card with author's name and shortened title.

(a)

> Watkins, Ernest. <u>The Cautious Revolution</u>: <u>Britain Today and Tomorrow</u>. New York: Farrar, Straus, 1950.
>
> ①

(b)

> Watkins, Alfred J. <u>The Practice of Urban Economics</u>. Beverly Hills: Sage Publications, 1980.
>
> ①

(c)

> Watkins, Alfred. <u>Practice</u>.
>
> ②

EXHIBIT 4.6   A card showing the correct pagination for source.

(p. 14) Watkins states: "Eliot's critical principles eliminated the poet from the poem — or at least excluded many aspects of the poet's whole being."

Summary:
> Contemporary American artists are more interested in the marketplace than their predecessors. They want people to buy as well as enjoy their works.

Paraphrase:
> Recently, American artists have become distrustful of the older notion that good artists must not be concerned with the commercial value of their art. Indeed, they themselves have become sales representatives for their own material. They enjoy going public and have become much more interested in public relations than were those artists who preceded them.

The direct quotation is sixty-six words; the summary, twenty-three; the paraphrase, fifty-five. Moreover, the summary and paraphrase capture the tone as well as the gist of the contents—in this case, a tone of worry that artists may be a little too interested in the business of art rather than in art itself. To summarize a quotation, read it and then put the note card aside for a few moments before writing the information in your own words.

Although you should summarize whenever possible, there are times when it is necessary to quote directly or to blend paraphrase with direct quotation. Directly quote

1. when you have no margin of error for accuracy, as with statistical data;

2. when you explain a complex or sophisticated process, as with a technical explanation of the function of microchips in the latest computer hardware;

3. when you especially are taken with a source's figurative or energetic style, as with Sir Winston Churchill's famous speeches to the British during World War II;

4. when you illustrate or interpret abstract or theoretical material, as with complicated, relatively subjective interpretations of theology or aesthetics.

Paraphrase when you feel it necessary to simplify but are fearful of oversimplification. Too much direct quotation may indicate that you have not understood your sources.

Punctuation and Direct Quotation:
Use double quotation marks with a quoted passage that you blend into your own sentence. For example, author Carey Lovelace states: "A new generation of American artists has rejected the modernist notion of art as a 'spiritual project' this in the words of Susan Sontag."

Single quotation marks in the above passage delineate a quotation within a quotation. Lovelace quotes Sontag and you must show this additional quotation.

If a passage is long (more than three typed lines), then you should block it to show direct quotation. To block a quotation, double space, indent ten spaces from the left margin, and type or print all the way to the right margin. Note, for example, the original quotation from "Painting for Dollars" in this chapter. Blocked quotations are not enclosed with quotation marks unless the source itself uses quotation marks. Also, note that quotations within blocked quotations take double marks, as with the phrase "spiritual project" in our first quotation from "Painting for Dollars."

Brackets and the Use of *sic*:
After you write a direct quotation on a note card, check carefully to make certain you have quoted accurately. If there is an error in the source, you should quote the error, as well as the rest of the passage, exactly as you find it. After the error, place the underlined or italicized Latin word *sic* (meaning *thus it is*), to indicate that you found the error in the source but that it is not your error. Do not use parentheses; use brackets only. For example,

"Log houses are becomming [*sic*] popular once again,' says a local real estate brochure."

The word *becoming* is misspelled, but you would quote it the way you find it and use the word *sic* with brackets.

Also use brackets, not parentheses, to add clarifying information or your own data to a direct quotation. For instance, in the following directly quoted sentence the researcher adds a word to clarify a pronoun's reference:

> "It [the seaplane] even can land in small lakes or ponds."

Quote dialogue or conversation exactly as you find it, without the use of *sic,* even though the dialogue may be ungrammatical or dialectical.

Lengthy explanations of a concept, word, or phrase that may be unfamiliar to your reader are best defined or explained in a footnote or endnote rather than with brackets in the quotation. This practice helps to ensure coherent sentence structure and paragraph unity.

Ellipses:
If you choose to leave out parts of a directly quoted passage, show this omission by the use of ellipses (three spaced dots). For example:

> Carey Lovelace says that "a new generation of American artists has rejected the modernist notion of art as a 'spiritual project'. . . ."

The fourth dot is the period. If you do not need a period, use only three dots. Place a period at the end of your sentence even after ellipses, and indicate periods left out of quoted material with four dots rather than with three. Ellipses at the beginning of a blended quotation are unnecessary, for it is obvious that you are using part of a passage in this case. For example, you would not state the following:

> Carey Lovelace says that " . . . a new generation of American artists has rejected the modernist notion of art. . . ."

The first ellipsis is not needed.

Plagiarism:
All paraphrases and all direct quotations must be documented. You must always credit the ideas of others, even if you do not directly quote them. Plagiarism, presenting the thoughts or data of others as your own, is a serious offense and may destroy a researcher's credibility and reputation. Also recall that the documented ideas of experts strengthen your own arguments.

Step 4: Linking the Notecards and the Outline

After you have outlined the structure of your paper (see Chapter 6), you should reread all note cards to determine their functions in the first draft. As you determine the exact function of each note, catalogue each card, using the top line—the red one—to link the card and outline. Refer to Exhibits 4.7 and 4.8 for examples.

When you have assigned each card to a section of your outline, order all IA's, IB's, etc., into their proper sequence and begin to write your paper starting with all cards marked IA.

Step 5: Arranging Notecards for a Bibliography

During the course of writing your paper, do not discard any note cards. Keep cards that you have chosen not to use. For the final stage of the paper—the bibliography—also depends on some of these cards. When you are ready to write the bibliography, simply take all cards labeled number 1, arrange them in alphabetical order by authors' last names, and copy the bibliographical entries already on the back of these cards for your paper's bibliography.

Following these five steps will lead you to a logically organized, accurately documented research paper.

EXHIBIT 4.7 A card linked to the outline and indicating the first reference to Lovelace.

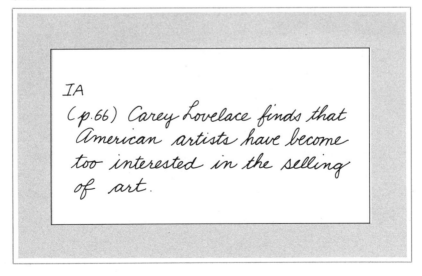

IA
(p.66) Carey Lovelace finds that American artists have become too interested in the selling of art.

EXHIBIT 4.8   Card with another reference to Lovelace, linked with a later section of the outline.

IV B

(p. 68) Lovelace states: "As the 1970's wore on the basic contradictions under-lying all their activity could not be avoided - these antiobject, antiaudience, anti-institution works of art were being subsidized by the very corporations, museums, and government bodies they were in theory meant to undermine."

EXERCISES

1. Explain in your own words the meaning and the implications of plagiarism.

2. List the ways to avoid plagiarism.

3. Photocopy a short article listed in the *Reader's Guide to Periodical Literature* and paraphrase one paragraph from the article.

4. Check the article and list what you consider to be general information.

5. Write a short paragraph summarizing the content of the article.

CHAPTER 5

EVALUATING THE EVIDENCE

After the initial work of gathering the evidence, you must evaluate it. During this second major stage of research, you must become very familiar with all data or information and remain thoroughly objective regarding its appropriateness. You must decide which, if any, evidence is convincing enough to present in a research paper. To prove your case, your careful evaluation of the evidence is just as important as the painstaking gathering of the evidence. You continually should evaluate evidence as you do your preliminary reading as well as during the outlining process.

The first step in evaluating evidence is to decide if it is primary or secondary. Primary sources are hard, raw data—first-hand, factual information. Consider this evidence as more trustworthy than secondary material. Secondary sources are reports, articles, books, or other observations that draw conclusions based on primary material. To the historian, for instance, personal letters written by soldiers in the Civil War are primary sources. Books based on these letters, such as Bell I. Wiley's *The Life of Johnny Reb* and *The Life of Billy Yank,* are secondary sources. A poem or painting is a primary source for the literary scholar or art critic; an article interpreting a poem or painting, a secondary one. For the sociologist, primary sources might include data from a statistically valid questionnaire; secondary sources, others' generalizations about the responses to the questionnaire. Most scholars and librarians consider initial publication of experimental data in the professional literature as primary sources in the sciences. A good research paper or report is a careful blend of both primary and secondary sources. That is, it reflects a knowledge of both raw data and others' thinking about that data.

Primary sources, like basic economic statistics, are readily available in most libraries through various government publications, weekly magazines, and economic journals. However, many college and public libraries may not be adequate reservoirs of primary evidence for other kinds of research. Actual experimental data on the chemical reduction of PCB's to harmless salts probably is unavailable to many of us. Nevertheless, articles on the subject are plentiful, and you may write a very interesting research paper on this very significant and timely subject while using only secondary sources. Such a report never would be accepted by a scientific journal as an adequate research project, but it could be quite informative for a lay audience. A newspaper article such as "PCB's Taken to the Cleaners in Atlanta," *The Florida Times-Union and Jacksonville Journal* 26 June 1983, could prove to be a productive starting point for the venture. In short, a very meaningful research paper also might be a comprehensive survey of secondary material already published on the subject.

The Importance of Dates

A survey of secondary sources on this topic or almost any other scientific topic necessarily must reflect the latest laboratory research. Basic scientific research aided by state-of-the-art technology expands primary knowledge in geometric proportion each year. You must always pay careful attention to the date of your sources as you evaluate their usefulness. This principle applies especially to scientific and technological topics, but is hardly limited to them. A later historian who has access to new information might write a more accurate account of an event than an earlier one with limited information. While a more recent date does not mean necessarily a more accurate, more knowledgeable, more useful article or book, the date of either primary or secondary research on any topic must be considered as a major standard of evaluation.

The Importance of the Medium

In addition to the date of your source, you must consider its medium. While newspaper reportage on PCB's may prove to be very informative and a good starting point for your research, you would find articles on PCB research that are published in scientific journals to be more factual, thorough, and trustworthy. The medium of research often does send a message. To cite only newspapers or popular magazines in a paper on PCB research would be to confess to a shallow job of research. Using the reference hints provided in Chapter 3, try to cite articles from reputable academic journals in your own research project.

Books: Some Special Considerations

Not only should you carefully evaluate kinds and sources of articles and essays, you also should consider several other standards of evaluation for books on your subject. After considering the original copyright date of a book, see if it has been revised at a later date. Use only the latest, revised editions. They usually have been corrected for errors from previous editions and contain updated material. Moreover, you should consider a book's publisher. Remember that not all books are created equal. Some are published by scholarly presses (often university presses), some by trade presses, and some by authors themselves through subsidized presses (called vanity presses). Books published by vanity presses may be poorly researched, but you cannot be certain; some may prove to be useful. In general, reliability of information ranges in declining order from scholarly presses to trade presses to vanity presses. If possible, check information in a book published by a vanity press against that found in other sources to see if other scholars support its conclusions. University and trade presses submit manuscripts to knowledgeable readers for evaluation and analysis before accepting them for publication. Furthermore, university presses are most likely to publish research for a limited readership.

Often a researcher finds the sheer number of books with possibly useful information to be overwhelming. Many veteran researchers suggest two ways to solve this problem. The first method is to peruse reviews of the book for summaries of their contents and general conclusions. Check your library reference shelf for the *Book Review Digest,* mentioned in Chapter 3. This resource actually quotes parts of the reviews and may prove to be the most helpful. Other good sources of reviews are the *Index to Book Reviews in the Humanities* and the *Book Review Citation Index.* A good rule in using any of these resources is to start with the reviews that are cited in academic journals. They usually are written by experts in the fields under consideration, and they often have greater depth and breadth than those in popular magazines or newspapers. The notable exceptions are *The New York Review of Books* and *The New York Times Book Review.*

A second way to solve the problem of the sheer numbers of possibly useful books is to check their indexes for entries on your subject. If you only scan their table of contents, which give broad chapter headings, you risk missing important information. Catchy, fancy chapter headings may not be good indicators of content. Take the few extra minutes to check a book's index for specific information.

Many instructors also recommend that the novice researcher take an author's reputation into account when evaluating a book's evidence. In general, this probably is a good idea; nevertheless, it often works better in theory than in practice for two reasons. First, an author's reputation itself might not be easily evaluated. Scholars themselves have subjective difficulties evaluating the work of their colleagues. Entries in various biographical dictionaries (see Chapter 3) certainly give accurate data such as academic training, experience, and publications. Yet, one must remember that scholarly reputations change, often dramatically, with growing bodies of knowledge. Secondly, reputations do not invariably indicate comprehensive, valid research. Recently, Emory University's prestigious School of Medicine retracted some articles written by a heart specialist whose reputation had blossomed. His work apparently was flawed and perhaps even fraudulent. Scholarly reputation is of some importance; it is not of prime importance in the evaluation of evidence.

Still another principle of evaluation of sources is to check to see if information in one source is validated or corroborated by information in other sources. Also, by reading an author's notes and bibliography, you can see readily if he or she draws from a general body of knowledge. Be wary of sources that do not have references to past scholarship. Probably no item of information should be included in your paper *as solid evidence* if it is supported by only one source. If you can find only one source, say so. Then qualify accordingly any generalization based on only one source, saying that you are presenting it for the reader's information and judgment, and that it might be questionable.

CHAPTER 6

WRITING THE PAPER

While you are in the process of examining the various sources that you select to be the basis for your paper, you will begin to discover ways that your information can be organized. Once you begin to see the direction your paper will take, you should write a general, informal outline for the paper. This outline will help you find possible weaknesses in your own thoughts or a lack of thoroughness in your research that might cause your final paper to lack balance and objectivity. By finding the weaknesses early, you may avoid having to make additional trips to the library after you have begun writing the first draft of your paper.

Once you have completed your research and feel reasonably certain you have all or at least most of the information you will need, the next step is to prepare a formal outline. In some cases, your instructor may want to examine your outline so that he or she can suggest ways to improve your paper. For this reason, you should try to make your outline as complete as possible so that only small changes must be made. However, even at this stage be prepared to make changes in your outline. Read your notes carefully until you thoroughly understand the material you have gathered and have a clear plan for presenting what you have in the best possible way.

A good outline is essential for a clear presentation. From your outline, your instructor usually can tell whether or not you understand your subject and have presented your material effectively. A good outline will simplify the writing of the paper and help to ensure logical clarity.

When you structure a formal outline, think in terms of pairs—no I without a II, no A without B, no 1 without 2. This time-honored system forces you to develop fully your ideas in concrete detail.

Not	*But*
I.	I.
A.	A.
II.	B.
A.	II.
B.	A.
III.	B.
A.	III.
1.	A.
	1.
	2.
	B.

The more detailed the outline is, the more thoughtful and convincing the paper will be. Moreover, the paper will be much easier to write if most of the illustrative details are already in place in the outline. Each major heading of a good outline expands the scope of the paper; each subheading provides a narrower, more manageable focus of the broader idea.

However, you must never enslave yourself to the mechanics of outlining or to the outline itself. Always give an idea a chance to grow, a chance to illuminate another idea. A good outline should be fertile ground for new perspectives and revisions. Outlining, like the actual composition of the paper, is a process. It should be open to revision at any stage of planning or execution.

Outline Formats

There are two general types of formal outlines: topic outlines and sentence outlines. In most instances, your instructor will specify which one to employ. Before turning in the final version of your paper, you should be certain that you are using the correct type. Both types list major ideas and subordinate ideas in a logical order of presentation.

In topic outlines, headings and subheadings usually are expressed in similarly constructed phrases—not in complete sentences. Sentence outlines, on the other hand, call for complete sentences for both headings and subheadings. Sentence outlines invariably require more detailed thought and preparation.

You should adopt the convention of using parallel construction in either type of outline not only for the appearance of stylistic symmetry and order, but also for the discipline it imposes. That is, parallel construction encourages you to think more precisely and concretely and to consider possible qualifications with greater deliberation. Also, parallel construction itself illustrates ideas of equal significance.

Begin your outline with the title of the paper, which you should center on the page. Capitalize the major words in the title just as you would in the titles of themes or essays. Immediately below the title and beginning at the left margin, you should state the thesis for your paper. In your outline, you may shorten the thesis statement as long as you do not alter the basic ideas that will appear in the thesis paper itself. Next comes the formal outline. (See Exhibit 6.1.)

The Introduction and the Conclusion

You should take special care when composing both the introduction and the conclusion. Your first and last impressions on the reader

Exhibit 6.1 An example of a skeleton for a formal outline.

Title of Paper

Statement of Thesis

  I. The first major section of the paper

    A. The first point related to I

    B. The second point related to I

      1. Information supporting IB, but not of equal importance

      2. Information supporting IB, but not of equal importance

  II. The second major section of the paper

    A. The first point related to II

    B. The second point related to II

    C. The third point related to II

are extremely important in both content and tone. A good introduction should state clearly your main theme in a clear thesis sentence, and it also should establish a tone of objectivity and assurance. Flowery rhetoric and emotional bombast are inappropriate for unbiased research papers, especially for introductions and conclusions.

The conclusion should do more than merely summarize factual data or restate a thesis statement. An effective conclusion reminds the reader *why* and *how* a definitive statement may be reached; it does more than just make a statement. More importantly, it does not introduce a new topic. It either resolves differing arguments or tells why they cannot be resolved conclusively. Never attempt to expand the paper thematically in its conclusion.

Supporting Examples

Documented examples usually are necessary for every major generalization in your paper. Rarely can generalizations stand on their own. They need concrete, detailed examples to be truly convincing (hence, the necessity of detailed outlines). The outline is the place to remind yourself of specific examples to use in key places, usually

Exhibit 6.2   A sample topic outline.

**William Randolph Hearst's Initial Involvement
in the Spanish-American War**

Thesis Statement: Publishing tycoon William Randolph Hearst encouraged prowar sentiments in the months before the outbreak of the Spanish-American War.

I. Problems with circulation and Hearst's reporting of the conflict

   A. Hearst's personal role in biased reporting

   B. Hearst's profits from war

II. Background of New York Journal immediately prior to support of Cuban cause

   A. Endorsement of William Jennings Bryan

      1. Support of William Jennings Bryan only partial

         a. Income tax

         b. Corporate regulation

      2. No support for Bryan's position on free silver

      3. The only major Eastern newspaper to endorse Bryan

   B. Effect of endorsement of Bryan on Journal

      1. Increased circulation

      2. Brought Journal close to financial ruin

      3. Made Hearst search for issues to provide profits

III. Approach of Journal to Cuban insurrection

   A. Initial events

      1. Provided public with flood of articles, cartoons

         a. Portrayed Spanish as tyrants

         b. Portrayed Cubans in substandard living conditions

      2. Allowed only one-sided articles

         a. Some true

         b. Some fabricated

      3. Became only source for information on Cuba

         a. To American people

         b. To American government

B. Remington's reporting

  1. Reported "no war"

  2. Told to stay by Hearst—war would be furnished

C. Evangelina Cosio y Cisneros's story

  1. Journal's articles identified her

    a. Daughter of President of Cuban Republic

    b. Prisoner—accused of helping set up capture of Spanish military leader

  2. Journal's appeals to readers to petition Spain for Evangelina's release

    a. Many women joined

    b. First Lady and others joined

  3. Journal's circulation grows

  4. The petition fails

  5. Journal correspondent sent to arrange release

    a. Decker's success

    b. Diplomatic furor

    c. Increased circulation

  6. Swanberg's quotation to summarize furor

D. Maine's explosion

  1. Cause unknown

  2. Exploitation by Hearst

    a. Journal's headlines accusing Spanish

    b. Extra issue

    c. Inflammatory photographs

    d. Printed war games

  3. Circulation increased

  4. Involvement of Hearst in explosion of Maine?

    a. Senate investigation

    b. Links to Cuban junta in New York City

    c. Support of Hearst for Cuban junta

IV. Profitability of war for Hearst

A. Circulation increased

B. Profits for Journal

in the numbered subsections below the main divisions of the outline. Recall that every subsection of the outline should narrow the more generalized focus of the headings. Detailed examples help focus your own ideas, and thus your reader's, on the topic at hand.

Presenting Other Opinions

You should not hesitate to include well documented, opposing views in your paper. The inclusion of differing opinions, in fact, strengthens your statement of your own opinion because it reveals depth and breadth of research; careful analysis of various perspectives; and an unbiased, objective tone.

Two sample research papers follow, one on a historical topic, the other on a literary one. The first paper is preceded by illustrations of topic and sentence outlines and the second by a sentence outline. Also, several pages of both sample papers are annotated with examples and brief discussions of structural and stylistic strengths and weaknesses.

Exhibit 6.3   A brief example of a sentence outline.

> I. Hearst's New York Journal suffers from declining circulation in the prewar months.
>   A. Hearst sees the diplomatic problem between Spain and Cuba as a chance to increase circulation.
>   B. Patriotic motives aside, Hearst greatly profits from the war.

① If your instructor requires a title page, make sure that the title and the other data are centered and balanced. Remember that this title page will be your reader's first impression of your work.

William Randolph Hearst's Initial Involvement ——— ❶

In the Spanish-American War

Legia M. Bennett

English 102

Professor Williams

(2) Center your title at the top of page 1. Allow enough space for all margins. Triple space above and below the title. Double space the paper.

(3) The introduction clearly states the main topic: Hearst's journalism encouraged war with Spain.

(4) Place all periods and commas inside quotation marks, unless the period follows the reference in parentheses. Note that documentation follows the style of the *MLA Handbook* (1984). See page 122 for additional examples.

(5) To indicate italics underline the title of works published separately, such as *New York Journal.* Use quotation marks for works published as part of other works, such as articles in periodicals. Note one exception: the books of the Bible, such as Genesis and Romans, do not require underlining or quotation marks.

(6) The assertion that Hearst's *Journal* was in financial trouble needs no documentation because it was found in several different sources. Thus, it is considered common knowledge.

(7) Page 1 needs no page number.

William Randolph Hearst's Initial Involvement
In the Spanish-American War

The journalism of William Randolph Hearst clearly helped
to mold public opinion to support war with Spain in 1898.
While one scholar's assertion that "without W. R. Hearst
there would have been no Spanish-American War . . ."
(Winkler 97) may be exaggerated, Hearst did rally public
opinion that favored the war. Furthermore, evidence
indicates that Hearst and his New York Journal profited
greatly from the events that led to the United States'
involvement in the Cuban conflict with Spain, although the
newspaper was almost bankrupt before the conflict.

In the year 1896, Hearst chose to back William Jennings
Bryan as a Democratic nominee for president of the United
States. Mr. Bryan campaigned heavily on the issue of a free
silver economy. Although W. R. Hearst did not support free
silver, he openly supported Bryan in his Journal. As W. A.
Swanberg states, "He was in accord with Bryan in his
espousal of the income tax and the regulation of railroads
and corporations. But he considered Bryan dead wrong on
the silver plank, which was the overriding issue of the
campaign" (101). The New York Journal was the only major
Eastern newspaper to support Bryan as a presidential
candidate. This had an unusual effect on the Journal, for it
increased its circulation while losing it money (Swanberg
103). Hearst's Journal continued to support Bryan and to lose
money until some were afraid of its financial ruin. Being the
publishing genius that he was, Hearst foresaw the need for
an issue to increase the Journal's circulation along with its

8   Beginning with page 2, paginate all pages in the upper right hand corner.

9   Note that the name *Frederic* is in brackets; it is not in parentheses. When you need to add information to a direct quotation, use brackets only. If your typewriter or word processor will not print brackets, draw them in by hand.

10   Note the use of documented evidence to back up generalizations such as Hearst's journalistic propaganda about the oppressed Cubans. Here and elsewhere a direct quotation from a primary source such as Hearst's *Journal* would have strengthened this student's argument. However, when primary sources are unavailable, use secondary ones (in this case Winkler and Swanberg) to illustrate generalizations.

11   Use the present tense when introducing most direct quotations (e.g., "As John K. Winkler states . . .").

2

profits. The Cuban insurrection was just the issue Hearst
needed.

Hearst immediately demanded the recognition of Cuba as an
independent state. "The Journal published stories illustrated by
detailed drawings of [Frederic] Remington showing Spanish
atrocities committed in Cuba" (Winkler 98). The Cuban
insurrection got the American public's interest away from Mr.
Bryan, and his eventual defeat, and onto the Cubans' struggle
for independence. The Journal began to provide its readers with
articles, pictures, and cartoons depicting the Spanish in Cuba as
inhumane tyrants. Americans were led to believe that living
conditions in Cuba were substandard and that the Cuban people
were greatly oppressed by their Spanish conquerors. The
columns of Hearst's Journal flourished with articles about
Cuba's plight, some real, some mere fabrications. As John K.
Winkler states, "For the first time in a matter of National
importance, Hearst demonstrated the preponderant effectiveness
of intelligently directed newspaper propaganda" (97). Hearst
made the American public believe exactly what he wanted them
to by publishing only the articles that would strengthen his
position and increase the circulation of his Journal. And W. A.
Swanberg adds: "Most ironic of all, the United States
administration, which had to base top-level policy on the facts of
the Cuban situation, knew scarcely more than was printed in the
newspapers" (139). Swanberg finds that our government officials
had little more information to go by on the Cuban crisis, than
what they read in the newspaper. Hearst was able to influence
United States policy.

⑫ Material such as the quoted telegrams used here are probably available to most students from secondary sources such as Winkler. Quote from primary sources when possible. If it is not possible, quoting from secondary sources is acceptable.

⑬ Does the story of Evangelina Cosio y Cisneros need an introductory transition? Do not forget to provide adequate transition between paragraphs as well as within them. For example, in this case the student might have said: "To help furnish newspaper copy for his private journalistic war, Hearst happily turned to the rather poignant story of a Spanish prisoner named Evangelina Cosio y Cisneros. Evangelina's story came to Hearst's attention in the fall of 1897."

⑭ Who is General Wyler? All names that would be unfamiliar to your reader need some introduction.

3

When events in Cuba seemed relatively quiet, Frederic Remington, the Journal's Cuban correspondent, sent the following ironic telegram to Hearst: "'Everything is quiet. There is no trouble here. There will be no war. I wish to return'" (Winkler 95). And Hearst allegedly replied, "'Please remain. You furnish the pictures and I'll furnish the war.'" Hearst commenced to accomplish exactly what he vowed. "In the United States, public indignation and circulation boomed simultaneously" (Winkler 95).

In the fall of 1897, the fate of Evangelina Cosio y Cisneros was brought to the attention of Hearst. She was a very beautiful, seventeen-year-old Cuban girl, said to have been related to the president of the Provincial Cuban Republic. The Spanish accused Cisneros of luring Colonel Jose Berriz, a Spaniard, and setting him up to be seized by three Cuban political prisoners. After a proper trial, General Wyler sentenced her to Casa de Recojidas, a Spanish prison. "Her unhappy fate attracted W. R. Hearst, proprietor of the New York Journal, and he, actuated no doubt by philanthropic motives, as well as the desire to advance the interests of his own paper, determined to make an effort for her release" (White 294). Hearst published a series of articles appealing to the women of the United States to form a petition to the Queen of Spain pleading for this young girl's release. Many prominent American women, including the first lady, joined in the crusade to save Miss Cisneros from her horrible plight. Once again Hearst's circulation grew.

⑮ Note the use of ellipses (three dots) to indicate material excluded from a direct quotation.

⑯ Twice now this student has mentioned that Hearst's overt support for the war increased the *Journal's* circulation. But this paper would be strengthened with some illustrative primary evidence of this increase— actual circulation totals.

⑰ Block relatively long quotations. Note that quotation marks are not used with blocked quotations except to show dialogue or to indicate quoted material within the blocked quotation.

4

After the petition to release Cisneros failed, Hearst took it upon himself to send a correspondent, Karl Decker, to provide Cisneros with a way of escape. Decker was successful in rescuing Miss Cisneros and bringing her safely back to the United States. Hearst had outstepped his legal limitations as a journalist when he inspired Cisneros' rescue. The October 12, 1897 issue of The New York Times states: "invasion of Havana by our contemporary's agent was perfectly indefensible, . . . and Spain must demand satisfaction or admit that her judges and officers were mediating an atrocious crime" (6). Many began to speculate that Spain had actually allowed the Journal to carry out its rescue of Cisneros. By October 14, 1897, The New York Times reported that "W. J. Calhoun of Danville, Special Commissioner to Cuba, knows enough on the political situation on that island to warrant his belief that Spanish authorities winked at the escape of Senorita Cisneros from a Havana prison. It released the authorities from an unpleasant situation without loss to their pride" (12). Whatever the circumstances surrounding her rescue, Hearst was able to arouse public interest and once again gain circulation for his Journal. Swanberg summarized the situation well when he wrote

> The Cisneros exploit improved the climate for war in three ways:
>
> 1. It gave millions of Americans a false impression of Spanish brutality in Cuba.
> 2. It showed the weakness of the President, the Secretary of State, and other officials in approving an illegal act insulting to Spain.

(18) Underline the names of ships, aircraft, and trains.

(19) Here the actual use of exact figures (3,098,825 copies) reinforces the argument with hard data.

5

3. It made millions of sensitive Spaniards hate the United
States. (7)

On February 16, 1898, Hearst's dreams were fulfilled. It was
on this date that the United States' battleship <u>Maine</u> exploded in
the harbor of Havana. Although the actual causes of the
explosion aboard the <u>Maine</u> are still not known today, W. R.
Hearst immediately began to print headlines implying that the
Spanish were responsible. This is exactly what Hearst had been
waiting for; some claim that he might have been behind it,
although no one really knows what the actual cause was. "On
February 20, 1898, the first Sunday extra of an evening
newspaper showed a two-page illustration purporting to show
'How the <u>Maine</u> Actually Looks As It Lies, Wrecked by Spanish
Treachery in Havana Bay.' Circulation for the three days
following the loss of the <u>Maine</u> totaled 3,098,825 copies, setting
a new all time mark for an American newspaper" (Winkler 104).
The <u>Journal</u> went as far as inventing war games and asking
readers for suggestions on how to get the war off to a good start
(Swanberg 173). The <u>Journal</u>'s circulation continued to increase
as the American public looked forward to war with Spain.

Later Senate investigations showed a possible connection
with the explosion of the <u>Maine</u> and the Cuban junta located in
New York City. Hearst was an outspoken supporter of the junta,
backing the Cuban independence movement any way he was able
to. <u>The New York Times</u> claimed: "Mr. Bennett announces
himself as an inventor of explosives and tells how he was called
upon by Gonzalo de Tuesado, Horatio S. Ruebens and others of
the Cuban junta in New York, who were greatly interested in his

⑳ Note that single quotation marks are employed for quotations within quotations.

㉑ Who is Pulitzer? Why is he mentioned? The student should have supplied some relevant information.

㉒ This conclusion is relatively weak because it relies too much on secondary material. If possible, your conclusion should be your own. It should indicate that you have synthesized both primary and secondary evidence into your own generalizations. For example, compare the following revision of the conclusion:

> Truly Hearst's journalistic war with Spain was very profitable for the *New York Journal.* Circulation increased dramatically in proportion to the newspaper's pro-war propaganda. Not only did Hearst fight his private journalistic war with Spain; he also triumphed in his war with other major newspapers which did not support the war. Almost simultaneously with the *Maine's* destruction came a tremendous surge in Hearst's newspaper circulation. Ignoring objective reporting and even personally interfering with United States foreign policy, Hearst promoted both the war and the profitability of his newspaper.

Note also that a good conclusion never raises new issues. An assertion that Hearst's brand of journalism died in the twentieth century, for example, would be out of place in this conclusion.

6

explosives, which he says 'emit light and flame and have four——⟨20⟩
times the strength of gunpowder.'" ("Cubans" 4).

"The <u>Maine</u> represented the fulfillment not of one want but
two—war with Spain and more circulation to beat Pulitzer"
(Swanberg 162). At the time war was declared with Spain, "the——⟨21⟩
total circulation of New York's pro-war newspapers was
1,560,000 against the anti-war total of 22,500" (138). Truly,——⟨22⟩
Hearst's war with Spain was extremely profitable to his <u>New
York</u> <u>Journal</u>.

(23) Unless your instructor prefers another term, label your bibliography *Works Cited*. Center the term at the top of the page; then triple space before the first entry. Paginate this page as well.

(24) Cite all sources that you have actually used in the paper. List them in alphabetical order with the authors' last names given first. Following the style of the *MLA Handbook* (1984), double space within entries and between entries. However, some instructors prefer single spacing within entries.

(25) A pictorial history usually is not preferred. Try to use a standard history for historical data. However, information available in this particular pictorial history makes it a valuable source. See Chapter 7 for additional examples of bibliographical entries. Note the use of the abbreviation *n.p.* (no place) when the place of publication is unavailable. Use *n.d.* for no date.

Works Cited

"Cubans and the Maine." New York Times 3 April 1898: 4, col. 2.

"Miss Cisneros Summoned." New York Times 14 October 1898:
7, col. 4.

Swanberg, W. A. Citizen Hearst. New York: Bantam Books, 1963.

"Topics of the Time—Personal." New York Times 12 October
1897: 6, col. 5–6.

White, Trumbull. Pictorial History of Our War With Spain for
Cuba's Freedom. N.p.: Freedom Publishing Co., 1898.

Winkler, John K. William Randolph Hearst: A New Appraisal.
New York: Hastings House, 1955.

Exhibit 6.4   An outline for a literary paper

Outline

I. Matthew Arnold develops a generally humanistic idealism.

   A. Goethe correctly diagnosed the ills of his age.

   B. Arnold, following Goethe, became a prophet of his era.

      1. He understood the malaise of Victorian England as basically a cultural and religious problem.

      2. He sought a cure in humanism.

         a. One should pursue culture for practical ends.

         b. Criticism is a divine calling, for it constructively enlarges one's vision of society.

   C. Arnold's idealism is not naive.

      1. He actually inspected many schools, at home and abroad.

      2. He acknowledged that culture was not confined to the intelligentsia.

      3. He believed that criticism was the duty of all human beings.

      4. He felt that humanity should strive for perfection.

      5. His hope is both an ancient and a modern goal.

II. Arnold hoped to achieve social perfection through education.

   A. He defended literature.

      1. Literature enlarges sympathy.

      2. It has humanizing power.

   B. But the essence of culture and humanism may not be tied to books.

   C. Arnold rejected "fixed systems."

      1. Class divisions of society are detrimental.

      2. Political change is necessary.

D. He had four major goals for studying.

   1. Study increases intelligence.

   2. Study trains all men to all that is human.

   3. Study helps one distinguish beauty from ugliness.

   4. Study should ideally humanize both knowledge and students.

E. He realistically saw challenges to his idealistic goals for education.

   1. English society reflected a cultural dichotomy.

      a. It was labor as toil.

      b. It believed literature was mere amusement.

   2. Some scholars relate Arnold's prophetic criticism to post-industrial America.

      a. Leisure is the center of life.

      b. Literature and art are escapes from rather than shapers of work.

III. Arnold believed that a reformed religion is necessary to humanize society.

   A. Religion needs to be demythologized.

      1. An unchanged religion will lose hold on people.

      2. People will lose spiritual perception.

      3. Religion must not fight scientific advancement.

   B. Religion's insights are poetic.

      1. God is an impersonal force.

      2. The purpose of religion is to motivate ethical conduct.

      3. Religion upholds psychological truths.

IV. Arnold sees his own ideas as in process.

   A. His and others' ideas are forever growing and organically changing.

   B. Continuing quest for ideas is a key to Arnold's humanism.

   C. Search for perfection leads to humanized society.

      1. Arnold does not lionize man.

      2. Man will not be impeded by false concepts in religion or philosophy.

This topic, which deals with literature, religion, education, and culture, is obviously more abstract than the topic of the previous paper. It requires presenting and analyzing ideas rather than historical events and documents. Structurally, it also requires a constant effort to maintain unity, for unlike the previous topic, it does not readily identify itself with definite historical events or chronological parameters. In this kind of abstract paper, an idea may easily lead to another less relevant idea. A major problem for this student, then, is to give adequate social context for Matthew Arnold's ideas without digressing from those ideas.

Matthew Arnold's Humanized Society———————————①

Rose Mary I. Foncree

English 300

Professor Marks

② Note that a verse quotation of more than three lines should be blocked, that is, it should begin as a new line, ten spaces from the left margin, double spaced.

③ What does "increase in civilization" exactly mean? The student should have defined the term for us.

④ Note that this student does define one of her main concepts, civilization, an abstract label which means different things to different people, that is, she gives Arnold's own working definition, which is even more helpful.

Matthew Arnold's Humanized Society

In his "Memorial Verses" written in 1850, Matthew Arnold
looks back to the time of Goethe, the near-golden age when the
great German poet

> took the suffering human race, ——————————②
>
> He read each wound, each weakness clear;
>
> And struck his finger on the place,
>
> And said: Thou ailest here, and here! (482)

In the same way, Arnold, both prophet and critic of his own day,
understood the spiritual and intellectual malaise that was
robbing society of its rightful humanity, and he sought a cure
for this cultural "dis-ease" in the propagation of "an inward
spiritual activity, having for its characters increased sweetness,
increased light, increased life, increased sympathy" (Culture and
Anarchy 515); in short, Arnold believed that a humanized society
would make man healthy and whole, that is, fully human.

Yet it was not culture alone that suffered for want of
humanization; man himself, by virtue of his religious and
intellectual dullness, had strayed far from the truly Christian
ethos and needed the corrective of a modern understanding of
religion in order to reshape his fundamental institutions,
namely the church and the school. For Arnold the proper way to
apply this corrective was through an increase in civilization, a ——————③
concept he defined as "the humanisation of man in society, the
satisfaction for him, in society, of the true law of human nature"
("Civilization" 352). As Michael Fischer points out, Arnold ——————④
longed to see in his own day a revival of civilized society, "a
society in which the free and flexible yet highly serious pursuit
of culture would inform practical activity" (93). Matthew

⑤ Generalizations (e.g., "Arnold was no idealistic dreamer") are bolstered with illustration, such as this account of Arnold's studies of the schools. They are also supported by quotation of knowledgeable secondary sources. Note, for instance, the quotation from Trethewey's work.

⑥ Use rhetorical questions sparingly. This student answers her own question, or better yet, allows her subject (Arnold) to answer it.

⑦ Again, one must define abstract terms like *culture* or at least offer another person's good working definition. Also mark the necessity of defining common terms like *criticism* when they are used in special ways.

2

Arnold was no idealistic dreamer; he worked assiduously at the uninspiring task of inspecting schools, and as Douglas Bush observes, he knew "the England of the middle and lower classes far better than his arm-chair critics" (6). Thus Arnold has been spared a number of the baleful attacks made against other intellectuals, particularly those of the "ivory tower" sort. In the twentieth-century meaning of the term, Arnold was a "working man," and in Eric Trethewey's cogent phrase, he knew "the gnosis of real experience grounded in the actual world" (21). It was this deeply human experience of involvement in the real world of work, sorrow and play that Arnold was concerned to see ennobled through the acquisition of what he called "Sweetness and Light" (Culture and Anarchy 512).

For Arnold, the so-called "Apostle of Culture," it was the milieu in which men found themselves that most clearly exhibited an undeveloped (if not truncated) humanity. Could man, though human by nature, retain his innate humanity in a society which one writer describes as basically hostile to human enterprise because it is so indifferent to, if not outright belligerent of, art? (Fisher 90). An appreciation of art in a humanized society is of the first importance, for art can make a civilization "interesting," that is, distinctive and beautiful ("Civilization in the United States" 358).

In his great essay Culture and Anarchy, Arnold defines culture as "a study of perfection" (508); it is culture which "places human perfection in an internal condition, in the growth and predominance of our humanity proper" (509). It is just here, in culture's search for human perfection, that the critic finds his rightful place. Indeed, it is Arnold's classic

8 Repetition of phrases can provide good transition between paragraphs. The phrase "thrill of awe" is effectively repeated here.

9 Often you may wish to repeat briefly an important working definition. For example, this student repeats Matthew Arnold's definition of *culture* ("study of perfection") just as a useful reminder.

10 Block quotations of prose that are more than four typed lines. Remember that parenthetical documentation of a blocked quotation follows the period.

3

definition of criticism that lifts the need for a discerning scrutiny of society to something like a diverse calling. Criticism, in Arnold's words, is "a disinterested endeavor to learn and propagate the best that is known and thought in the world" ("Function of Criticism" 507). True criticism (not to be confused with the critical spirit which can be damaging rather than constructive) is a <u>wholly</u> constructive attempt to enlarge the vision and mission of society. It is an essentially human endeavor, and is worthy, therefore, of both honor and respect. Yet the function of criticism is not confined, according to Arnold, to the so-called intelligentsia; rather, the critic is a thoughtful human being who seeks the culmination of perfection in human society, the person who seeks what Goethe called "the thrill of awe," for awe "is the best thing humanity ——————⑧ has" ("Civilization in the United States" 360).

   If the "thrill of awe" is to be valued and sought after, so much more ought humanity to long for "Sweetness and Light," for such longing will show an understanding of the "essential character of human perfection" and will produce a society like that of ancient Greece—a society of "immense spiritual significance" (<u>Culture</u> <u>and</u> <u>Anarchy</u> 512). In such a society this "Sweetness" or aesthetic appeal (beauty) will be in a harmonious relationship with the "Light" or understanding (intelligence) of its human inhabitants. According to Arnold, then, culture, the "study of perfection," will produce not anarchy (the state of ——————⑨ confused, ugly disorder) but the beauty of a new golden age, an age rife with artistic pleasure and accomplishment:

      Again and again I have insisted how those are the happy ——————⑩
      moments of humanity, how those are the marking epochs

11 Use exclamations sparingly, if at all. Perhaps a declarative sentence here would have implied less emotional involvement.

12 Is this lamentation of contemporary scholar Douglas Bush justified? Is it digressive? Yes and no. Here the student wishes to validate Arnold's ideas and criticism about education with modern illustrations because Arnold himself had the future in mind.

4

of a people's life, how those are the flowering times for
literature and art and all the creative power of genius,
when there is a national glow of life and thought, when the
whole society is in the fullest measure permeated by
thought, sensible to beauty, intelligent and alive. Only it
must be real thought and real beauty; real sweetness and
real light. (Culture and Anarchy 517)

What a remarkable breadth of vision for mankind's fractured,
warring society! It would be unreasonably naive to credit
Arnold's great vision of culture humanized and refined to a
hopelessly optimistic Victorian outlook; his longing for a
renewed golden age of literature is as ancient as Homer and as
modern as a contemporary critic who, in commenting on
Arnold's desire for an educated populace, writes that "television
and rock music have engendered hordes of bookless, mindless
youth," and illiteracy rather than literacy is the thing of the day
(Bush 11).

It is in just such a bookless society that Arnold's faith in the
value of literature may seem the most foolish. In describing
Arnold's view of literature in the spread of culture, Eric
Trethewey writes that Arnold believed

the course of knowledge for people in modern society, the
instrument of enlarging their sympathies and perceptions
was to be the vicarious experience of books. . . . He had the
conviction, shadowed by grave doubts in our time, of the
efficacy of literature as a humanizing power. (20)

Yet Arnold, while at heart a humanist and a believer in

13 Underline foreign phrases such as *raison d'etre.*

14 Use brackets, not parentheses, to add explanatory material within a direct quotation.

5

humane letters, does not confuse vital living with the mold and dust of books. According to Trethewey, he knew that "all human knowing is existential. . . . The best that has been thought and said, does not derive ultimately from books or dogmatic principles" (20). Arnold's view of culture (and criticism), in fact, may in essence have little or nothing to do with books. Park Honan mentions that a great deal of misunderstanding of Arnold is due probably more to his critics than to his readers, for it is they (the critics) who have not been as careful as they should have been in presenting a clear headed notion of Arnold's concepts. This is especially true, Honan believes, with regard to his supposed efforts toward a high culture, one whose very raison d'etre would be the publishing, disseminating, and reading of books (and more books). Honan insists that this view is simply untrue, for "in the 'Preface' to his first edition Arnold insists that those who have never read books may enter into this condition [that of "culture"], which involves a growing, a becoming. . . . The process may involve a rejection of books, and always involves rejection of faith in fixed systems and shibboleths" (6).

Arnold's own rejection of "fixed systems" is shown in his belief that a society structured on class divisions was an obstacle to man's full humanization. Michael Fischer points out that Arnold was discerning enough to see that it would take more than literature to thwart the degrading influences of the class society of his day; he believed, in fact, that it would take not only the exercise of criticism and the achievement of public education, but also the intervention of political mandate (97). In

(15) Note how an introductory adverbial clause ("Although ... Arnold knew ...") can provide effective transition between paragraphs.

(16) Placing Arnold in the company of other social critics is more than academic name dropping, for Arnold places himself in a certain tradition. The documentation for the comparison is to Arnold's own works.

6

his essay "Civilization in the United States" Arnold credits the apparently natural grace of American women with their freedom from class division; he describes the American woman's free and happy manner as giving "pleasure," and he notes that such a national characteristic is "undoubtedly, a note of civilization; and an evidence, at the same time, of the good effect of equality upon social life" (357).

Although, as mentioned above, Arnold knew that the Sweetness and Light of culture could not come about solely through criticism and education, education was, nevertheless, a subject that occupied a remarkable amount of his time and thought, not to say his writings. True to his essential humanism, Arnold believed, along with Montesquieu, that "the first motive which ought to impel us to study is the desire to augment the excellence of our nature, and to render an intelligent being yet more intelligent" (Culture and Anarchy 508). He saw education as an indispensable aid in bringing about a more "human" race; as a matter of fact, he quotes approvingly the "excellent maxim" of the seventeenth-century Moravian schoolmaster John Comenius who taught that "the aim [of education] is to train generally all who are born men to all which is human" ("Elementary Education" 29).

This goal of humanness in education suffuses Arnold's writings on the subject; in the essay "Common Schools Abroad," Arnold observes:

> Surely, to be offended by ugliness, to be delighted and
> refreshed by beauty, is eminently human; just as, on the
> other hand, it is a proof that our humanity is raw and

15

16

⑰ Arnold's idealism here is presented as representative of Victorian idealism in general. The generalization is not left hanging; the quotation from Peter Burnham, a secondary source, lends credence to it.

⑱ What is meant by "human system of education"? One is not sure, even after reading Arnold's own words from "Elementary Education." A brief definition might be helpful.

7

undeveloped if we confound the two together or are
indifferent to them. (89)

That education is peculiarly susceptible of interpretation by the
vagaries of idealism is widely known, and Arnold has been
accused of excessive idealism just here. Yet, as Peter Burnham
observes, Arnold's idealism, while being perhaps "specifically
Victorian in that it emphasizes the struggle toward perfection,"
is idealism of the sort the Victorian society of Arnold's day
admired; it was, after all, "only a very callous and blunt 'shabby
fellow' [who] could possibly be satisfied with the status quo"
(18). Like the great German critics Lessing and Herder whom he
admired, Arnold wished to humanize knowledge. He writes that
those persons will be remembered throughout human posterity
who have "humanized knowledge," who like Lessing and Herder
"broadened the basis of life and intelligence; because they
worked powerfully to diffuse sweetness and light" (<u>Culture and
Anarchy</u> 518).

Arnold longed to see a profoundly human system of
education. He was particularly fond of the German schools,
believing them to be far superior to the British system. In his
"Elementary Education" he writes:

> But the higher one rises in a German school the more is
> the superiority of the instruction over ours visible. Again
> and again I find written in my notes, <u>the children human</u>.
> They had been brought under teaching of a quality to
> touch and interest them, and were being formed by it. (28)

19 The statement, "The cultural dichotomy inherent in our . . . society," begs for concrete definition and gets it.

20 The commentary on American society is not digressive because Arnold himself—as evident in the paper—often compared and contrasted the American and British societies.

8

Aside from his optimism and hope that the teaching of literature would help bring about a "national glow," Arnold realized the probability of challenges to his humanistic concepts. In his fine essay "Matthew Arnold's Anticipation of Subsequent Challenges to Humanism," Michael Fischer analyzes the historical and cultural development from the time of Arnold to the present. He shows that the cultural dichotomy inherent in our English (and American) society, that is, Hebraism on the one hand and Hellenism on the other, had tended to split society just at this point, for "labor and literature had split apart; the one had become brutalizing toil and the other inconsequential amusement" (90). According to Fischer, this situation exists to the present day, for we live in a "post-industrial America" where leisure rather than work is the center of our social and national life. As a consequence, literature and art (the humanities) "have acquired a deceptive prominence in these persons' lives as pastimes which assuage rather than shape what they do in their work" (87).

If education was of central importance in the "humanisation of man in society," of still greater importance was religion. In Culture and Anarchy Arnold describes religion as "the greatest and most important of the efforts by which the human race has manifested its impulse to perfect itself—religion, that voice of the deepest human experience" (509). For Arnold, a view of religion demystified and stripped of supernaturalism would ensure man's continued intellectual and spiritual progress. He abhorred so-called "slaughter-house" religion which saw a dying Jesus save the world. Such mythology, according to Arnold, could serve only to delay the coming of humanism to religion; he

21   Because Arnold's views of religion are complex and unorthodox, this student wisely relies on direct quotation rather than on summary or paraphrase.

22   Personal interruptions such as, "nor will he be the last," are best avoided.

9

foresaw the time when such religion as existed in the churches would lose its hold on people, and, in the absence of anything better or truer, they would lose their spiritual perception. Sensing the mood of scientific distrust of the miraculous, Arnold writes that the

> immense, the epoch-making changes of our own day, a stage in our intellectual development [that] is now declaring itself when mythology, whether moral or immoral, as a basis for religion is no longer receivable, is no longer an aid to religion but an obstacle. Our own nation is not specially lucid, it is strongly religious, we have witnessed in the Salvation Army the spectacle of one of the crudest and most turbid developments of religion with the element of mythology in full sway; and yet it is certain that, even amongst ourselves, over all which is most vigorous and progressive in our population, mythology in religion has lost or is fast losing its power, and that it has no future. ("A 'Friend of God'" 185)

Arnold was not the first—nor will he be the last—to predict the imminent demise of religion, but he was an astute observer of the contemporary scene and believed that it was mainly the established religion (the Church of England) which fought every advance of scientific fact or inquiry. He considered it a positive duty for the churchman to be willing to accept and praise every advance of science. Leslie Brisman comments:

> It is Arnold's special message for his time that the more scientific our perspective about our creaturely origins, the stronger our faith in creative rebirth ought to be. Every discovery about the evolution of man from lower animals

23 This paragraph could use clarification. Are the emotive terms like "mumbo-jumbo" and "God talk" Arnold's or the student's? One is never sure.

24 A reader is sure of Arnold's general intentions as a critic of Victorian religion, for they are stated clearly and logically in an item in series, an excellent illustration of stylistically effective summary.

25 Here the student mentions a false charge against Arnold—that he attempted to substitute poetry for religion. Perhaps an explanatory footnote or endnote, a practice allowed by the *MLA Handbook,* (1984) would be useful here, without adding digressive material to the paragraph.

10

and the evolution of the Biblical canon from primitive
literary fragments ought to buttress our conviction that
what culture has won from nature we must not let go of
again. (8)

For the average man or woman on the street, however, how
was this to be done? Certainly not by reading one's Bible in the
traditional way. Arnold knew that if ever there would come about
a renewed Christianity, it must come dressed in different
clothing. The old modes of thinking, the worn out cliches, the
whole bag of mumbo-jumbo that made up "God-talk" must be
thrown out. What the church needed was not only a renewed
consciousness but a revamped Lord and a revised edition of a
book that had outlived its theological usefulness. What Arnold
sought to do was to take a long, hard look at religion, identify its
cultural and historical weaknesses (particularly Christianity as
interpreted by Victorian England), and through an updated
hermeneutic give it a renewed vitality, perhaps even a new image
completely. He set about doing this in Literature and Dogma,
"the work of Arnold's that caused the most stir in his own
time," and which has "lost the most ground since then" (Bush
2). In this complex essay Arnold enlarges upon the theme that
Christianity's failure has been primarily one of linguistic
inaptitude, that is, the church has failed to understand the
language of the Bible; it was "misunderstood because its
language was regarded as being scientific or metaphysical rather
than poetic" (Trethewey 7).

There can be little doubt that Arnold did not attempt (as some
have charged) to substitute poetry for religion; it was, however,
as Gerold Savory observes, Arnold's desire to demonstrate that

㉖ Another footnote or endnote explaining who comprises "the great school of demythology of our own day" might be useful.

11

religion's most valid and lasting insights <u>are</u> in poetry.
Thus, their power to inspire and console rests upon man's
capacity for "imaginative reason," that faculty Arnold
found often lacking but, nonetheless, crucial in the
modern mind's search for guideposts in the wilderness.
(21)

What Arnold was attempting to do for religion was nothing
more nor less than a monumental feat: a demythologizing of the
Biblical narrative while poeticizing its meaning. Understand-
ably, Arnold's work as a theologian has been severely criticized.
In a number of ways he foreshadowed, as Savory points out, the
great school of demythology of our own day (16); on the other
hand, a number of critics have charged that his concept of
religion is "wholly inadequate for its complete want of any real
intellectual bracing" (Creevy 136).

David DeLaura notes that we ourselves are now living in the
"secular and religionless future" that Newman foresaw in the
1870's at the time Arnold published his <u>Literature</u> <u>and</u> <u>Dogma,</u>
and he writes that it was just "here in the 1870's we can detect
one of the great shifts in modern culture, and in the history of
human imagination" (3). This shift away from biblical revelation
and authority to scientific procedure and speculation was at the
heart of Arnold's desire to refashion Christianity into a
philosophy more attractive to modern, intelligent men. That
Arnold may have misjudged the intellectual stature of
individuals of past ages is beside the point; he felt keenly the
impingement of the modern era upon his own. He believed the
most logical action was neither hostility toward the spirit of the
age nor fear of the truth, but an updating of old patterns of
thinking.

26

27 Again, if one's subject requires special usages for common words, carefully present them (e.g., Arnold's usage for "divine").

28 The student here mentions the rise of a new orthodoxy which found Arnold's ideas to be "superficial optimism." The inclusion of the opinions of Arnold's detractors strengthens this paper. One knows that the writer of this paper is familiar with other opinions of Arnold's work; thus, her own opinions mean more.

12

For Arnold the Bible is divine, but, as Eric Trethewey explains, this conception of "divinity" did not mean to Arnold that Christianity's sacred book is in any sense supernatural or miraculous (7). Indeed, the very words "supernatural" and "miraculous" are completely out of place in the Christian vocabulary because God is not a "superperson who 'loves and thinks'" (Brisman 2–3). As Trethewey observes, Arnold comes finally to the conclusion that God is an "impersonal force in the universe," that everlasting phenomenon of power outside of our own selves which creates the power of righteousness in us (8). Indeed, Arnold describes God's intuited voice as the "collective voice of the best men thinking their best thoughts" (Trethewey 8). It seems clear that Arnold did not intend to be misunderstood on this point, and that he did intend sensible individuals to consider seriously his demythologized God.

What Arnold could not have foreseen, of course, was the rise of a new supernaturalism and a renewed orthodoxy some seventy-five years or so in the future, an orthodoxy whose adherents would consider his theological concepts the product of a brilliant mind infused by a superficial optimism. Peter Burnham remarks that Arnold's view of religion was completely existential for "he simply does not believe in an after-life or a transcendent realm in any literal sense. . . . Everything must be achieved here on earth, or it will not be achieved at all" (18). Still, one can find little fault with a man who felt as keenly as Arnold did the value of some kind of faith in society's struggle toward perfection and humanization, for he knew that the purpose of religion was "conduct" and that conduct was "three-fourths of life" (Literature and Dogma 175).

(29) Note again the necessity of direct quotation rather than summary or paraphrase when discussing complex concepts, such as Arnold's usage of the common term *facts*.

(30) Should this student be apologetic in her conclusion? Actually she *has* shown the complexity of Arnold's mind. Such apologies might be construed as false modesty, but, more importantly, they might undermine confidence in an otherwise well researched paper.

13

When Matthew Arnold looked around him and saw what he perceived to be the theologically-destructive achievements of modern science, he came to the conclusion that a credible apologetic of traditional Christianity (which he felt to have been emptied of all cultural relevance) would "have to be based on something more solid than either supernaturalism or scientific rationalism" (Savory 20). What he wished to base such a defense on were what he called the "facts." As Gerold Savory explains, by the "facts" he

> meant more than just the cold data of scientific research. There are psychological "facts" as well, and the truth of an emotionally verifiable experience carries just as much weight as the truth of a logically verifiable argument. Indeed, it appears to carry even more weight; for, although Arnold is a rationalist, he is also a poet, and his unique contribution to nineteenth-century biblical criticism was that he brought an aesthetic viewpoint to his reevaluation of Christian ethics and to his study of the Bible. (20–21)

In a brief study it is impossible to show in any detail the human complexity of a deep literary and philosophical thinker like Matthew Arnold. One can simply scratch the surface of so great a personality and stand in amazement of both the scope of his contribution to English literature and the depth of his human wisdom. As Park Honan points out in an open letter to the The <u>Arnoldian</u>, Arnold is as fascinating a writer for our own day as any of our contemporaries, but we must be careful to avoid over-interpretation of this great Victorian:

> In one popular essay after another, in book-reviews,
> lectures, guidebooks, or surveys relating to Arnold and the

31 This conclusion nicely summarizes Arnold's basic precepts and ideas without being unduly redundant.

14

Victorians, in our time, we read or hear that Arnold's "idea" of religion or poetry or education "was" this or that. Arnold becomes a pudding; we dip out of him anything we like. . . . The Arnold who lived from 1822 to 1888 had no "idea" about anything, but a developing idea or a set of ideas, often involving interesting contradictions. . . . [T]his movement or continual quest in his thought, along with his habit of avoiding definitions and looking for infrastructures, makes him interesting today. (7)

This quest or development which Honan describes as being part of Arnold's character is a clue to his deep humanism. Growth into full humanity involves development, maturation, change; it is a fully human, fully rational process. Arnold believed that in order for inherently rational man to achieve full humanity, he must seek after perfection, the imbuing of his culture with "Sweetness and Light." In Arnold's view man becomes fully human in a society that neither mythologizes or lionizes him, but one in which his unique humanity is given full rein to strive toward perfection, unimpeded by misguided religious or philosophic concepts that tend ultimately to dehumanize him.

31

32 The "Works Cited" section should begin on a new numbered page.

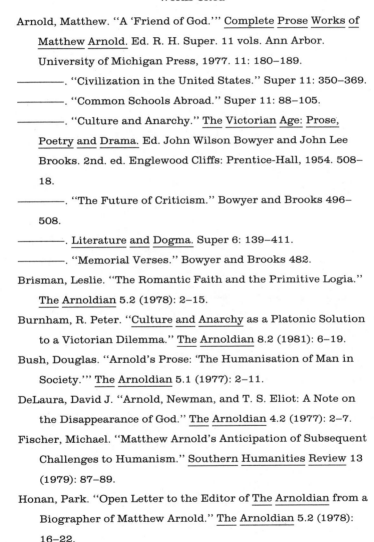

15

Works Cited

Arnold, Matthew. "A 'Friend of God.'" Complete Prose Works of
Matthew Arnold. Ed. R. H. Super. 11 vols. Ann Arbor.
University of Michigan Press, 1977. 11: 180–189.

————. "Civilization in the United States." Super 11: 350–369.

————. "Common Schools Abroad." Super 11: 88–105.

————. "Culture and Anarchy." The Victorian Age: Prose,
Poetry and Drama. Ed. John Wilson Bowyer and John Lee
Brooks. 2nd. ed. Englewood Cliffs: Prentice-Hall, 1954. 508–
18.

————. "The Future of Criticism." Bowyer and Brooks 496–
508.

————. Literature and Dogma. Super 6: 139–411.

————. "Memorial Verses." Bowyer and Brooks 482.

Brisman, Leslie. "The Romantic Faith and the Primitive Logia."
The Arnoldian 5.2 (1978): 2–15.

Burnham, R. Peter. "Culture and Anarchy as a Platonic Solution
to a Victorian Dilemma." The Arnoldian 8.2 (1981): 6–19.

Bush, Douglas. "Arnold's Prose: 'The Humanisation of Man in
Society.'" The Arnoldian 5.1 (1977): 2–11.

DeLaura, David J. "Arnold, Newman, and T. S. Eliot: A Note on
the Disappearance of God." The Arnoldian 4.2 (1977): 2–7.

Fischer, Michael. "Matthew Arnold's Anticipation of Subsequent
Challenges to Humanism." Southern Humanities Review 13
(1979): 87–89.

Honan, Park. "Open Letter to the Editor of The Arnoldian from a
Biographer of Matthew Arnold." The Arnoldian 5.2 (1978):
16–22.

16

Savory, Gerold. "The Gospel According to Arnold: <u>Literature and Dogma</u> and <u>God and the Bible</u>." *The Arnoldian* 5.2 (1978): 16–22.

Trethewey, Eric. "The 'Method of Jesus': Experience and the Moral Life in Matthew Arnold's Poetic Theory of Criticism." <u>The Arnoldian</u> 9.2 (1982): 6–21.

CHAPTER 7

DOCUMENTING YOUR
RESEARCH PAPER

- Purposes of Documention
- Documentation Guides
- The MLA Handbook for Writers of Research Papers (1984)
- The MLA Handbook for Writers of Research Papers, Theses, and Dissertations (1980)
- The APA Publication Manual
- Exercises

Your research paper will certainly include many of your own ideas. It will also include information that you have located in the published writings of other individuals or groups. Over the years, certain customs have developed in research writing that make it easy for you to designate the information in your paper which was actually located in other sources.

These documentation customs require that you add to your research paper a list of the sources you have used. This list of sources may be called Works Cited, or Bibliography, or References. You link these sources to specific areas of your paper by adding place markers within the text whenever material from a source was used to supply or document material in a particular sentence or paragraph. These place markers may consist of information contained within parentheses and added to the end of a sentence in your text, or they may be a series of numbers that direct the reader to notes placed either at the foot of a page (footnotes) or at the end of your paper (endnotes).

Documentation has three major purposes.

1. It allows you to give proper intellectual credit to a source while still incorporating the source's material in your paper.

2. It helps you support your own ideas with information from other authoritative sources. If you wrote that the economy of the United States is in danger because the inflation rate was 12.5% last year, your reader will tend to believe you if you indicate that the source of the inflation rate data was a publication of the U.S. Department of Commerce.

3. It assists your reader in locating more information on your topic. You may spend four weeks on a research paper, assembling a list of sources and writing the actual paper itself. Your reader can use your work to read about your topic and go directly to the sources of your information without having to spend time discovering them.

There are customary formats used for documentation. These standards usually contain rules and examples which will apply to any documentary situation, and your readers will be accustomed to the appearance of documentary information in this form.

Documentation Guides

Three widely used documentary guides are the *MLA Handbook for Writers of Research Papers* (New York: Modern Language Association, 1984); the *MLA Handbook for Writers of Research Papers, Theses, and Dissertations* (New York: Modern Language Association, 1980); and the *Publication Manual of the American Psychological Association* (Washington: American Psychological Association, 1983). For comprehensive information on any one of these documentary styles, you should consult the appropriate guide directly.

Examples of ten common documentary situations in each of the three styles are shown in the next section.

The MLA Handbook for Writers of Research Papers (1984)

The documentary style recommended by the *MLA Handbook* (1984) features a list of works cited, which appears at the end of the research paper. Whenever information from a specific work is used within the text, the page reference for that information will be added in parentheses. If the author or title of the source have not been identified in the text or are not clear from the context of the passage, these author and title elements may be added to the page reference within the parentheses. Complete documentation for each source is contained in the *Works Cited* portion of the paper.

Ten examples of documentation using the format of the *MLA Handbook* (1984) follow.

EXAMPLE 1   **A book with one author.**

> Ford, Robert N. Motivation Through the Work Itself. New York:
>
> American Management Association, 1969.

EXAMPLE 2   **A book with two or more authors.**

> Rosser, James M., and Howard E. Mossberg. An Analysis of Health
>
> Care Delivery. New York: Wiley, 1977.

EXAMPLE 3   **A book with an editor.**

> Mossman, Jennifer, ed. New Pseudonyms and Nicknames. Detroit:
>
> Gale Research Co., 1981.

EXAMPLE 4   A book with a corporate author.

National Education Association of the United States. Maximum
   Salaries Scheduled for Administrators. Washington: National
   Education Association of the United States, 1969.

EXAMPLE 5   A book with chapters by different authors.

Pedersen, Knud. "A New Middle Way in Scandinavia." The Nordic
   Model: Studies in Public Policy Innovation. Ed. Clive Archer and
   Stephen Maxwell. Westmead, England: Gower Publishing Co.,
   1980. 35–51.

EXAMPLE 6   An article in a reference work.

Switzer, George. "Cryolite." Encyclopedia Americana. 1980 ed.

EXAMPLE 7   A government publication.

U.S. Department of the Interior. Bureau of Land Management. Final
   Henry Mountain Grazing Environmental Impact Statement.
   Washington: GPO, 1983.

**EXAMPLE 8   An article in a periodical with continuous
             pagination.**

Brown, Laura. "The Ideology of Restoration Form: John Dryden."
   PMLA 97 (1982): 395–407.

EXAMPLE 9   An article in a periodical with separate pagination.

Lovelace, Richard. "Future Shock and Christian Hope." Christianity
   Today, 27.12 (1983): 12–16.

EXAMPLE 10   An article in a newspaper.

Hall, Trish. "For Trendy Dinners, Basil Is the Herb to Be Seen With."
   Wall Street Journal 12 Sept. 1983: 1.

The MLA Handbook for Writers of Research Papers,
Theses, and Dissertations (1980)

The style of documentation recommended by the *MLA Handbook*
(1980) features a full set of notes that are linked to the text by a

consecutive numbering system. The notes serve to designate each use of information from the various sources consulted by the researcher. Complete information about the sources themselves will be contained in a bibliography at the end of the research paper. Ten examples follow.

EXAMPLE 1   **A book with one author.**

Note:

> [1]Robert N. Ford, Motivation Through the Work Itself (New York: American Management Association, 1969), p. 201.

Bibliography:

> Ford, Robert N. Motivation Through the Work Itself. New York: American Management Association, 1969.

EXAMPLE 2   **A book with two or more authors.**

Note:

> [2]James M. Rosser and Howard E. Mossberg, An Analysis of Health Care Delivery (New York: Wiley, 1977), p. 33.

Bibliography:

> Rosser, James M., and Howard E. Mossberg. An Analysis of Health Care Delivery. New York: Wiley, 1977.

EXAMPLE 3   **A book with an editor.**

Note:

> [3]Jennifer Mossman, ed., New Pseudonymns and Nicknames (Detroit: Gale Research Co., 1981), p. 42.

Bibliography:

> Mossman, Jennifer, ed. New Pseudonymns and Nicknames. Detroit: Gale Research Co., 1981.

EXAMPLE 4   **A book with a corporate author.**

Note:

> [4]National Education Association of the United States, Maximum Salaries Scheduled for Administrators (Washington: National Education Association of the United States, 1969), p. 94.

Bibliography:

> National Education Association of the United States. <u>Maximum</u>
> <u>Salaries Scheduled for Administrators</u>. Washington: National
> Education Association of the United States, 1969.

EXAMPLE 5   A book with chapters by different authors.

Note:

> [5]Knud Pedersen, "A New Middle Way in Scandinavia," in <u>The</u>
> <u>Nordic Model: Studies in Public Policy Innovation,</u> ed. Clive Archer
> and Stephen Maxwell (Westmead, England: Gower Publishing Co.,
> 1980), p. 40.

Bibliography:

> Pedersen, Knud. "A New Middle Way in Scandinavia." In <u>The Nordic</u>
> <u>Model: Studies in Public Policy Innovation</u>. Ed. Clive Archer and
> Stephen Maxwell. Westmead, England: Gower Publishing Co.,
> 1980.

EXAMPLE 6   An article in a reference work.

Note:

> [6]George Switzer, "Cryolite," <u>Encyclopedia Americana,</u> 1980 ed.

Bibliography:

> Switzer, George. "Cryolite." <u>Encyclopedia Americana</u>. 1980 ed.

EXAMPLE 7   A government publication.

Note:

> [7]U.S. Department of the Interior, Bureau of Land Management,
> <u>Final Henry Mountain Grazing Environmental Impact Statement</u>
> (Washington, D.C.: GPO, 1983), p. 43.

Bibliography:

> U.S. Department of the Interior. Bureau of Land Management. <u>Final</u>
> <u>Henry Mountain Grazing Environmental Impact Statement</u>.
> Washington, D.C.: GPO, 1983.

EXAMPLE 8   **An article in a periodical with continuous pagination.**

Note:

[8]Laura Brown, "The Ideology of Restoration Form: John Dryden,"
PMLA, 97 (1982), 396.

Bibliography:

Brown, Laura. "The Ideology of Restoration Form: John Dryden."
PMLA, 97 (1982), 395–407.

EXAMPLE 9   **An article in a periodical with separate pagination.**

Note:

[9]Richard Lovelace, "Future Shock and Christian Hope,"
Christianity Today, 27, no. 12 (August 5, 1983), 13.

Bibliography:

Lovelace, Richard. "Future Shock and Christian Hope." Christianity
Today, 27, no. 12 (August 5, 1983), 12–16.

EXAMPLE 10   **An article in a newspaper.**

Note:

[10]Trish Hall, "For Trendy Dinners, Basil Is the Herb to Be Seen
With," Wall Street Journal, 12 Sept, 1983, p. 1, col. 4.

Bibliography:

Hall, Trish. "For Trendy Dinners, Basil Is the Herb to Be Seen With".
Wall Street Journal, 12 Sept. 1983, p. 1, col. 4.

The APA Publication Manual

The documentary style recommended by the *Publication Manual of the American Psychological Association* features a complete listing of all sources in a reference section of the research paper. As we have seen in the new *MLA* (1984) style, separate footnotes are generally not utilized to mark each occurrence of the incorporation of source material. Instead, parenthetical comments are inserted within the text to identify the item in the list of references that is being cited in that particular section of the research paper. Ten common documentary examples in the *APA Publication Manual* style follow.

EXAMPLE 1   A book with one author.

Ford, R. N. (1969). Motivation through the work itself. New York: American Management Association.

EXAMPLE 2   A book with two or more authors.

Rosser, J. M., & Mossberg, H. E. (1977). An analysis of health care delivery. New York: Wiley.

EXAMPLE 3   A book with an editor.

Mossman, J. (Ed.). (1981). New pseudonymns and nicknames. Detroit: Gale Research Co.

EXAMPLE 4   A book with a corporate author.

National Education Association of the United States. (1969). Maximum salaries scheduled for administrators. Washington: National Education Association of the United States.

EXAMPLE 5   A book with chapters by different authors.

Pedersen, K. (1980). A new middle way in Scandinavia. In C. Archer, & S. Maxwell, (Eds.), The Nordic Model: Studies in Public Policy Innovation (pp. 35–51). Westmead, England: Gower Publishing Co.

EXAMPLE 6   An article in a reference work.

Switzer, G. (1980). Cryolite. In Encyclopedia Americana (Vol. 8, p. 275). Danbury, Conn: Americana Corporation.

EXAMPLE 7   A government publication.

U.S. Department of the Interior. Bureau of Land Management. (1983). Final Henry Mountain grazing environmental impact statement. Washington, D.C.: U.S. Government Printing Office.

EXAMPLE 8   An article in a periodical with continuous pagination.

Brown, L. (1982). The ideology of Restoration form: John Dryden. PMLA, 97, 395–407.

EXAMPLE 9   **An article in a periodical with separate pagination.**

> Lovelace, R. (1983). Future shock and Christian hope. Christianity
>   Today, 27(12), 12–16.

EXAMPLE 10   **An article in a newspaper.**

> Hall, T. (1983, September 12). For trendy dinners, basil is the herb to
>   be seen with. Wall Street Journal, p. 1.

EXERCISES

Using the new *MLA* format, write bibliographical entries for each of the following:

1. a newspaper article about an election;

2. a magazine article in which the pagination is not consecutive;

3. a government publication;

4. a scholarly journal article in your major or about some subject that interests you;

5. a book written by two authors.

APPENDIX A

LIBRARY CLASSIFICATION SYSTEMS

- The Library of Congress Classification System
- The Dewey Decimal Classification System
- The Superintendent of Documents Classification System

The three most common classification systems used in college libraries are the Library of Congress classification, the Dewey Decimal classification, and the Superintendent of Documents classification. Although you do not need to understand the significance of each element in the call numbers from these classifications, it is helpful to know the meaning of the first characters. These characters correspond to the broad subject category of the item, and all other items in this category should be shelved near the call number you have selected. The meaning of the first characters in each of the three classification systems is given below.

The Library of Congress Classification System

Call Number Begins With	Item Subject
A	General works (such as encyclopedias)
B	Philosophy and Religion
C	History: Auxiliary Sciences
D	History: General and European
E	History: America
F	History: America
G	Geography, Anthropology, Recreation
H	Social Sciences
J	Political Science
K	Law
L	Education
M	Music
N	Fine Arts
P	Language and Literature
Q	Science
R	Medicine
S	Agriculture
T	Technology and Home Economics
U	Military Science
V	Naval Science
Z	Bibliography and Library Science

The Dewey Decimal Classification System

Call Number Begins With	Item Subject
0	General works
1	Philosophy and related subjects
2	Religion
3	Social sciences
4	Language
5	Pure sciences
6	Applied sciences
7	Arts
8	Literature and rhetoric
9	Geography and history

The Superintendent of Documents Classification System

Unlike the classification systems outlined above, the first element of the Superintendent of Documents Classification is related not to the subject of the item but to the government agency which was responsible for the particular work.

Call Number Begins With	Item Published By
A	Agriculture Department
C	Commerce Department
CAB	Civil Aeronautics Board
CC	Federal Communications Commission
CR	Civil Rights Commission
CS	Civil Service Commission
D	Defense Department
ED	Education Department
EP	Environmental Protection Agency
FR	Federal Reserve System
GA	General Accounting Office
GS	General Services Administration
HH	Housing and Urban Development
I	Interior Department
J	Justice Department

Call Number Begins With	Item Published By
L	Labor Department
LC	Library of Congress
NA	National Academy of Sciences
P	Postal Service
PE	Peace Corps
PR	President of the United States
S	State Department
SI	Smithsonian Institution
T	Treasury Department
VA	Veterans Administration
X	Congress
Y	Congress

APPENDIX B

FIFTY TOPICS FOR RESEARCH PAPERS

1. Alcoholism: Is It a Disease?

2. AMX: Effective Missile System?

3. Apes: Can They Talk?

4. The Army: Volunteer or Conscription?

5. Athletic Scholarships: Opportunity or Exploitation?

6. Biofeedback: Science or Fiction?

7. Modern Theories of Continental Drift

8. Capital Punishment: Yes or No?

9. Child Abuse and the Courts

10. Cigarettes and Cancer: Proven Link?

11. ERA: Necessary or Unnecessary?

12. ESP: Fact or Fiction?

13. Euthanasia: Do We Have a Right to Die?

14. Freedom of Press *vs.* Gag Rules: Who Is Right?

15. Ethical Dilemmas of Genetic Engineering

16. Gold: Is It a Good Investment?

17. Gun Laws: Yes or No?

18. High School Illiterates: Has Public Education Failed?

19. Househusbands: Can Men Do the Job?

20. Jogging: Helpful or Harmful?

21. John F. Kennedy: Killed by One Man?

22. Whole Life Insurance: Is It Worth the Cost?

23. Mandatory Retirement: Should It Be Abolished?

24. Newspapers: Are They Becoming Too Commercial?

25. Large Budget Deficits: Harmful or Helpful?

26. Dilemmas of Nuclear Waste Disposal

27. Prisons: Do They Rehabilitate?

28. Sex Education: Does It Belong in Schools?

29. Social Security: Will It Be Solvent in 2000?

30. Solar Energy: Is It Practical?

31. Teenage Marriage: Inevitable Divorce?

32. Television News: Is It Entertainment?

33. Effects of Television Violence on Children

34. UFO's: Fact or Fiction?

35. The Unborn Fetus: Is It a Person?

36. Welfare: Social Benefit or Bane?

37. Women in Management: Effective or Ineffective?

38. Women Police Officers: Can They Do the Job?

39. Theodore Roosevelt as a Conservationist

40. The Nashville Agrarians as Social Critics

41. The Earliest Americans

42. Illegal Drugs and Professional Sports

43. Cocaine: A Major Threat to Good Health

44. Benefits of Genetic Research

45. Causes of Drought in North Africa

46. The Law and Teenage Offenders

47. Insanity Defense: Does It Need Modifications?

48. The Immigration Crisis in the United States

49. Acid Rain: Its Causes and Effects

50. The Great Ball Point Pen War of 1947–1950

APPENDIX C

LIBRARY REFERENCE SOURCES

- Art
- Biology
- Business
- Chemistry
- Communication Arts
- Computer Science
- Criminal Justice
- Education
- Engineering
- Geography
- Geology
- History
- Home Economics
- Language
- Law
- Literature
- Mathematics
- Medicine
- Music
- Philosophy
- Physics
- Political Science

- Psychology
- Recreation
- Religion
- Sociology

Chapter 3 contains a short list of books which will be helpful to you as you begin your search for information in your library. This appendix gives you a longer list of information resources in various subject areas to supplement the material in Chapter 3.

Did you know that there is a reference book called *The Encyclopedia of World Soccer?* If you were assigned a topic related to prisons, would the *Criminal Justice Periodicals Index* be helpful? Are you more eager to begin work on an obscure topic if you know that periodicals such as the *Journal for the History of Astronomy* and *The Journal of Popular Film* exist?

Each of the 26 subject areas presented in this appendix contains a list of the titles of reference books, periodical indexes, and periodicals which you could use as you expand your research activities beyond the fundamental sources listed in Chapter 3. The reference books may be encyclopedias, dictionaries, handbooks, guides to the literature, or introductory texts. The periodical indexes contain listings of articles in the periodicals of a certain subject area. The titles of the periodicals themselves should give you an appreciation of the great expanse of information contained in this type of material.

As you use this appendix, you should remember that your library may not contain all of the titles listed here. You may find earlier (or later) editions of a certain reference book. Subscriptions to scholarly periodicals are very expensive, and all libraries have budgetary limitations that control the number of periodicals they can afford to maintain. Regardless of the size of your library, however, it will have some specialized reference books, indexes, and periodicals available for your use. If you cannot find an item listed in this appendix, consult a librarian and ask for assistance in locating a similar title.

Your research paper will introduce your readers to *information* that will probably be new to them. Likewise, the research process itself will introduce you to many new *sources* of information. Do not be intimidated by the long lists of titles in this appendix. The fact that these specialized sources *exist* should give you confidence that you can successfully locate information on your topic in your library.

Art Books

Allep, Marsha C. *Illustration Index.* 4th ed. Metuchen, NJ: Scarecrow Press, 1980.

Arntzen, Etta Mae, and Robert Rainwater. *Guide to the Literature of Art History.* Chicago: American Library Association, 1980.

Bachman, Donna G., and Sherry Piland. *Women Artists: An Historical, Contemporary, and Feminist Bibliography.* Metuchen, NJ: Scarecrow Press, 1978.

Baigell, Matthew. *Dictionary of American Art.* New York: Harper & Row, 1979.

Boger, Louise A. *The Dictionary of World Pottery and Porcelain.* New York: Scribners, 1971.

The Britannica Encyclopedia of American Art. Chicago: Encyclopedia Britannica Educational Corporation, 1973.

Campbell, James Edward. *Pottery and Ceramics: A Guide to Information Sources.* Detroit: Gale, 1978.

The Complete Encyclopedia of Antiques. Ed. L. G. G. Ramsey. New York: Hawthorne, 1962.

Doumato, Lamia. *American Painting: A Guide to Information Sources.* Detroit: Gale, 1979.

Ehresmann, Donald L. *Fine Arts: A Bibliographic Guide to Basic Reference Works, Histories, and Handbooks.* 2nd ed. Littleton, CO: Libraries Unlimited, 1979.

Ekdahl, Janis. *American Sculpture: A Guide to Information Sources.* Detroit: Gale, 1977.

Ellis, Jessie Croft. *Index to Illustrations.* Boston: Faxon, 1966.

Encyclopedia of Architectural Technology. Ed. Pedro Guedes. New York: McGraw-Hill, 1979.

Encyclopedia of World Art. New York: McGraw-Hill, 1959–68.

Gardner, Helen. *Art Through the Ages.* 5th ed. New York: Harcourt, 1970.

Goldman, Bernard. *Reading and Writing in the Arts.* Rev. ed. Detroit: Wayne State University Press, 1978.

Hall, James. *Dictionary of Subjects and Symbols in Art.* Rev. ed. New York: Harper & Row, 1979.

Holmes, Oakley N. *The Complete Annotated Resource Guide to Black American Art.* Spring Valley, NY: Black Artists in America, 1978.

Hunt, William Dudley. *Encyclopedia of American Architecture.* New York: McGraw-Hill, 1980.

Ketchum, William C. *The Catalog of American Antiques.* New York: Rutledge Books, 1977.

Mayer, Ralph. *A Dictionary of Art Terms and Techniques.* New York: Crowell, 1969.

McGraw-Hill Dictionary of Art. Ed. Bernard S. Myers. New York: McGraw-Hill, 1969.

Muehsam, Gerd. *Guide to Basic Information Sources in the Visual Arts.* Santa Barbara, CA: ABC-Clio, 1978.

The Oxford Companion to Art. Ed. Harold Osborne. Oxford: Clarendon Press, 1970.

Post, Chandler R. *History of European and American Sculpture from the Early Christian Period to the Present Day.* Cambridge: Harvard University Press, 1921.

Richardson, Edgar Preston. *Painting in America.* New York: Crowell, 1956.

Robb, David Metheny. *Art in the Western World.* 4th ed. New York: Harper, 1963.

Savage, George. *Dictionary of Antiques.* New York: Praeger, 1970.

Walker, John Albert. *Glossary of Art, Architecture and Design Since 1945.* Hamden, CT: Linnet Books, 1977.

Art Indexes and Periodicals

Art Index.
The American Art Journal.
American Artist.
Antiquities.
Architectural Design.
Architectural Digest.
Architectural Record.
Art Education.
Artforum.
Ceramic Review.
Design.
Journal of Glass Studies.
National Sculpture Review.
Shuttle, Spindle and Dyepot.
Stained Glass.
Studio International.

Biology Books

Abercrombie, Michael. *Penguin Dictionary of Biology.* London: Allen Lane, 1977.

Blake, Sidney Fay. *Geographical Guide to Floras of the World.* Washington: GPO, 1942–61.

Bottle, Robert Thomas, and H. V. Wyatt. *The Use of Biological Literature.* 2nd ed. Hamden, CT: Archon Books, 1971.

Burton, Maurice. *Systematic Dictionary of Mammals of the World.* 2nd ed. London: Museum Press, 1965.

CRC Handbook of Microbiology. 2nd ed. Cleveland: CRC Press, 1977.

Carleton, R. Milton. *Index to Common Names of Herbaceius Plants.* Boston: G. K. Hall, 1959.

Carpenter, John Richard. *An Ecological Glossary.* Norman: University of Oklahoma Press, 1938.

Compton's Dictionary of the Natural Sciences. Chicago: Compton, 1966.

De La Torre-Bueno, Jose Rollin. *A Glossary of Entomology.* Lancaster, PA: Science Press, 1937.

Ditmars, Raymond Lee. *The Reptiles of North America.* New York: Doubleday, 1936.

George, J. David. Marine Life: *An Illustrated Encyclopedia of Invertebrates in the Sea.* New York: Wiley, 1979.

Gleason, Henry Allan. *The New Britton and Brown Illustrated Flora of the Northeastern United States and Adjacent Canada.* New York: New York Botanical Garden, 1952.

Gray, Asa. *Gray's Manual of Botany.* New York: American Book Company, 1950.

Gray, Peter. *The Encyclopedia of the Biological Sciences.* 2nd ed. New York: Van Nostrand Reinhold, 1970.

Grzimek, Bernhard, ed. *Grzimek's Animal Life Encylopedia.* New York: Van Nostrand Reinhold, 1972.

Grzimek, Bernhard, ed. *Grzimek's Encyclopedia of Ecology.* New York: Van Nostrand Reinhold, 1976.

Grzimek, Bernhard, ed. *Grzimek's Encyclopedia of Evolution.* New York: Van Nostrand Reinhold, 1976.

Hall, Eugene Raymond, and Keith R. Kelson. *The Mammals of North America.* New York: Ronald, 1959.

Herald, Earl Stannard. *Living Fishes of the World.* Garden City, NY: Doubleday, 1961.

Hortus Third: A Concise Dictionary of Plants Cultivated in the United States and Canada. New York: Macmillan, 1976.

Howe, William H. *The Butterflies of North America.* Garden City, NY: Doubleday, 1975.

Jeffrey, Charles. *Biological Nomenclature.* 2nd ed. New York: Crane, Russak, 1977.

King, Robert C. *A Dictionary of Genetics.* 2nd ed. New York: Oxford, 1974.

Larousse Encyclopedia of Animal Life. New York: McGraw-Hill, 1967.

Leftwich, A. W. *A Dictionary of Zoology*. London: Constable, 1973.

Leviton, Alan E. *Reptiles and Amphibians of North America*. New York: Doubleday, 1971.

Oxford Encyclopedia of Trees of the World. Oxford: Oxford University Press, 1981.

Palmer, Ralph S. *Handbook of North American Birds*. New Haven: Yale University Press, 1962–76.

Pennak, Robert William. *Collegiate Dictionary of Zoology*. New York: Ronald, 1964.

Peterson, Roger Tory. *A Field Guide to the Birds*. 4th ed. Boston: Houghton Mifflin, 1980.

Preston, Richard J. *North American Trees*. Ames: Iowa State University Press, 1961.

Rehder, Alfred. *Manual of Cultivated Trees and Shrubs Hardy to North America*. 2nd ed. New York: Macmillan, 1940.

Rickett, Harold William. *Wild Flowers of the United States*. New York: McGraw-Hill, 1966–1973.

Singleton, Paul. *Dictionary of Microbiology*. New York: Wiley, 1978.

Smith, Roger C. *Smith's Guide to the Literature of the Life Sciences*. 9th ed. Minneapolis: Burgess, 1980.

Snell, Walter Henry, and Esther A. Dick. *A Glossary of Mycology*. Cambridge: Harvard University Press, 1971.

Steen, Edwin B. *Dictionary of Biology*. New York: Barnes and Noble, 1971.

Thomson, Arthur Landsborough, ed. *A New Dictionary of Birds*. New York: McGraw-Hill, 1964.

Tootill, Elizabeth, ed. *The Facts on File Dictionary of Biology*. 2nd ed. New York: Facts on File, 1981.

Biology Indexes and Periodicals

Biological Abstracts.
Biological and Agricultural Index.
Ecological Abstracts.
General Science Index.
American Birds.
American Journal of Botany.
American Naturalist.
Anatomical Record.

Animal Record.
Annals of Botany.
Audubon Magazine
The Auk.
Behavior Genetics.
BioScience.
Biochemical Journal.
Biochemistry.
Biology of Reproduction.
Evolution.
Genetics.
Journal of Biological Chemistry.
Journal of Biological Education.
Journal of Cellular Physiology.
Journal of Experimental Biology.
Journal of Experimental Botany.
Journal of General Physiology.
Journal of Heredity.
Journal of Herpetology.
Journal of Natural History.
Life Sciences.
Plant Physiology.
Quarterly Review of Biology.

Business Books

Accountants' Handbook. Ed. Lee J. Seidler, 6th ed. New York: Wiley, 1981.

Ammer, Christine. *Dictionary of Business and Economics.* New York: Free Press, 1977.

Amstutz, Mark R. *Economics and Foreign Policy: A Guide to Information Sources.* Detroit: Gale, 1977.

Ayer Glossary of Advertising and Related Terms. 2nd ed. Philadelphia: Ayer Press, 1977.

Badger, Ralph E. *The Complete Guide to Investment Analysis.* New York: McGraw-Hill, 1967.

Bannock, Graham. *The Penguin Dictionary of Economics.* London: Allen Lane, 1977.

Barton, Roger, ed. *Handbook of Advertising Management.* New York: McGraw-Hill, 1970.

Baughn, William Hebert. *The Bankers' Handbook.* Rev. ed. Homewood: Dow Jones-Irwin, 1978.

Benn, Alice E. *The Management Dictionary.* New York: Exposition Press, 1952.

Brownstone, David M. *Where to Find Business Information.* New York: Wiley, 1979.

Coldrick, A. Percy. *The International Directory of the Trade Union Movement.* New York: Facts on File, 1979.

Dartnell Personnel Director's Handbook. Ed. Wilbert E. Scheer. Chicago: Dartnell, 1969.

Davids, Lewis E. *Dictionary of Insurance.* 2nd ed. Paterson, NJ: Littlefield, Adams, 1970.

Demarest, Rosemary R. *Accounting: Information Sources.* Detroit: Gale, 1970.

Encyclopedia of American Economic History. New York: Scribner, 1980.

Encyclopedia of Auditing Techniques. Ed. Jennie M. Palen. Englewood Cliffs, NJ: Prentice-Hall, 1967.

Encyclopedia of Professional Management. New York: McGraw-Hill, 1978.

Encyclopedic Dictionary of Business Finance. Englewood Cliffs, NJ: Prentice-Hall, 1961.

Encyclopedic Dictionary of Systems and Procedures. Englewood Cliffs, NJ: Prentice-Hall, 1966.

Figueroa, Oscar. *A Business Information Guidebook.* New York: Amacom, 1980.

Fletcher, John, ed. *The Use of Economics Literature.* London: Butterworths, 1971.

Franklin, Jerome L. *Human Resource Development in the Organization: A Guide to Information Sources.* Detroit: Gale, 1978.

French, Derek. *Dictionary of Management.* New York: International Publications Service, 1975.

Gilpin, Alan. *Dictionary of Economic Terms.* 4th ed. London: Butterworths, 1977.

Giordano, Albert G. *Concise Dictionary of Business Terminology.* Englewood Cliffs, NJ: Prentice-Hall, 1981.

Graham, Irvin. *Encyclopedia of Advertising.* 2nd ed. New York: Fairchild, 1969.

Handbook of Accounting and Auditing. Boston: Warren, Gorham & Lamont, 1981.

Helpple, Charles E. *Research Guide in Economics.* Morristown, NJ: General Learning Press, 1974.

Hutchinson, William Kenneth. *American Economic History: A Guide to Information Sources.* Detroit: Gale, 1980.

Knox, Vera H. *Public Finance: Information Sources.* Detroit: Gale, 1964.

Kohler, Eric Louis. *A Dictionary for Accountants.* 5th ed. Englewood Cliffs, NJ: Prentice-Hall, 1975.

Kraus, Albert L. *The New York Times Guide to Business and Finance: The American Economy and How It Works.* New York: Harper and Row, 1972.

Lindermann, A. J. *Dictionary of Management Terms.* Dubuque, IA: W. C. Brown, 1966.

McGraw-Hill Dictionary of Modern Economics. Ed. Douglas Greenwald. New York: McGraw-Hill, 1973.

Munn, Glenn. *Encyclopedia of Banking and Finance.* 6th ed. Boston: Bankers Publishing Co., 1962.

Osler, Robert W. *Glossary of Insurance Terms.* Santa Monica, CA: Insurors Press, 1972.

Shafritz, Jay M. *Dictionary of Personnel Management and Labor Relations.* Oak Park, IL: Moore Publishing Co., 1980.

Shapiro, Irving J. *Dictionary of Marketing Terms.* 4th ed. Totowa, NJ: Littlefield, Adams, 1981.

The Stock Market Handbook: Reference Manual for the Securities Industry. Ed. Frank G. Zarb. Homewood, IL: Dow Jones-Irwin, 1970.

Wey, James B. *Investment Information: A Detailed Guide to Selected Sources.* Detroit: Gale, 1970.

Wortman, Leon A. *A Deskbook of Business Management Terms.* New York: AMACOM, 1979.

Zaremba, Joseph. *Statistics and Econometrics: A Guide to Information Sources.* Detroit: Gale, 1980.

Business Indexes and Periodicals

Business Periodicals Index.
Personnel Management Abstracts.
Public Affairs Information Service.
Academy of Management Review.
Accountancy.
The Accounting Journal.
Accounting Review.
Across the Board.
Administrative Science Quarterly.
American Banker.

American Economic Review.
Bankers' Magazine.
Barrons': National Business and Financial Weekly.
Business Economics.
Business History Review.
Business Week.
Federal Reserve Bulletin.
Finance.
Financial Management.
Forbes.
Fortune.
Harvard Business Review.
Industrial Relations.
Industrial and Labor Relations Review.
Internal Auditor.
Journal of Accountancy.
Journal of Accounting Research.
Journal of Advertising Research.
Journal of Advertising.
Journal of Business Research.
Journal of Business.
Journal of Economic History.
Journal of Management Studies.
Journal of Marketing Research.
Journal of Marketing.
Labor Studies Journal.
Management Science.
Nation's Business.
Personnel Journal.
Personnel.
Public Relations Journal.
Sales and Marketing Management.

Chemistry Books

Anthony, Arthur. *Guide to Basic Information Sources in Chemistry.* New York: Wiley, 1979.

Bottle, Robert Thomas, ed. *The Use of Chemical Literature.* 3rd ed. London: Butterworths, 1979.

The Condensed Chemical Dictionary. Ed. Gessner G. Hawley. 9th ed. New York: Van Nostrand Reinhold, 1977.

Daintith, John, ed. *The Facts on File Dictionary of Chemistry.* 2nd ed. New York: Facts on File, 1981.

Dictionary of Organic Compounds. 4th ed. New York: Oxford University Press, 1965.

Flood, Walter Edgar. *The Dictionary of Chemical Names.* New York: Philosophical Library, 1963.

Gordon, Arnold J., and Richard A. Ford. *The Chemistry Companion: A Handbook of Practical Data, Techniques and References.* New York: Wiley, 1972.

Hampel, Clifford A., and Gessner G. Hawley, eds. *The Encyclopedia of Chemistry.* 3rd ed. New York: Van Nostrand Reinhold, 1973.

Handbook of Chemistry and Physics: A Ready Reference Book of Chemical and Physical Data. Cleveland: Chemical Rubber Co., 1913.

International Encyclopedia of Chemical Science. Princeton: Van Nostrand, 1964.

Meites, Louis, ed. *Handbook of Analytical Chemistry.* New York: McGraw-Hill, 1963.

Mellon, Melvin Guy. *Chemical Publications, Their Nature and Use.* 4th ed. New York: McGraw-Hill, 1965.

Mellor, Joseph William. *A Comprehensive Treatise on Inorganic and Theoretical Chemistry.* London: Longmans, 1922.

Merck Index: An Encyclopedia of Chemicals and Drugs. Ed. Paul G. Stecher. 8th ed. Rahway, NJ: Merck, 1968.

Rappoport, Zvi. *CRC Handbook of Tables for Organic Compound Identification.* 3rd ed. Cleveland: Chemical Rubber Co., 1967.

Woodburn, Henry M. *Using the Chemical Literature: A Practical Guide.* New York: Marcel Dekker, 1974.

Chemistry Indexes and Periodicals

Chemical Abstracts.
General Science Index.
American Chemical Society Journal.
Analytical Chemistry.
Chemical Instrumentation.

Chemical Technology.
Chemical and Engineering News.
Chemistry.
Education in Chemistry.
Inorganic Chemistry.
Journal of Applied Chemistry and Biotechnology.
Journal of Applied Electrochemistry.
Journal of Chemical Education.
Journal of Chemical and Engineering Data.
Journal of Organic Chemistry.
Pure and Applied Chemistry.

Communication Arts Books

Aller, John Jeffrey, and Henry Lee Ewbank. *Handbook for Discussion Leaders.* New York: Harper, 1954.

Barnouw, Erik. *A History of Broadcasting in the United States.* New York: Oxford University Press, 1966–1970.

Brockett, Oscar G. *A Bibliographical Guide to Research in Speech and Dramatic Art.* Chicago: Scott, Foresman, 1963.

Bronner, Edwin. *The Encyclopedia of the American Theatre, 1900–1975.* New York: A. S. Barnes, 1980.

Brown, Les. *The New York Times Encyclopedia of Television.* New York: Times Books, 1977.

Cawkwell, Tim. *The World Encyclopedia of the Film.* New York: World, 1972.

Cheshire, David F. Theatre: *History, Criticism and Reference.* Hamden, CT: Archon Books, 1967.

Cinema: A Critical Dictionary. Ed. Richard Roud. New York: Viking Press, 1980.

Dyment, Alan R. *The Literature of the Film.* London: White Lion, 1975.

Elsevier's Dictionary of Cinema, Sound and Music. Amsterdam: Elsevier, 1956.

The Encyclopedia of World Theatre. New York: Scribner, 1977.

Gassner, John. *The Reader's Encyclopedia of World Drama.* New York: Crowell, 1969.

Glenn, Robert W. *Black Rhetoric: A Guide to Afro-American Communication.* Metuchen, NJ: Scarecrow Press, 1976.

Gordon, Thomas F. *Mass Communication Effects and Processes.* Beverly Hills, CA: Sage Publications, 1978.

Halliwell, Leslie. *The Filmgoer's Companion.* 3rd ed. New York: Hill and Wang, 1970.

Hansen, Donald A., and J. Herschel Parsons. *Mass Communication: A Research Bibliography.* Santa Barbara: Glendessary Press, 1968.

Hartroll, Phyllis. *The Oxford Companion to the Theatre.* 3rd ed. London: Oxford University Press, 1967.

Kent, Ruth K. *The Language of Journalism.* Kent, Ohio: Kent State University Press, 1971.

Kesler, Jackson. *Theatrical Costume: A Guide to Information Sources.* Detroit: Gale, 1979.

Klotman, Phyllis Rauch. *Frame By Frame: A Black Filmography.* Bloomington: Indiana University Press, 1979.

Lanham, Richard A. *A Handlist of Rhetorical Terms.* Berkeley: University of California Press, 1968.

Magill's Survey of Cinema. Ed. Frank N. Magill. Englewood Cliffs, NJ: Salem Press, 1980.

Mott, Frank Luther. *American Journalism: A History, 1690–1960.* 3rd ed. New York: Macmillan, 1962.

Moving Pictures: An Annotated Guide to Selected Film Literature. South Brunswick, NJ: A. S. Barnes, 1979.

The Oxford Companion to Film. Ed. Liz-Anne Bawden. New York: Oxford University Press, 1976.

Price, Warren C. *The Literature of Journalism, An Annotated Bibliography.* Minneapolis: University of Minnesota Press, 1959.

Samples, Gordon. *How to Locate Reviews of Plays and Films.* Metuchen, NJ: Scarecrow Press, 1976.

Speech Association of America. *A History of Criticism of American Public Address.* New York: McGraw-Hill, 1943–1955.

Sutton, Roberta Briggs. *Speech Index.* 4th ed. New York: Scarecrow Press, 1966.

Taylor, J. R. *The Penguin Dictionary of the Theatre.* Baltimore: Penguin, 1966.

Whalon, Marion K. *Performing Arts Research: A Guide to Information Sources.* Detroit: Gale, 1976.

Wilmeth, Don B. *American and English Popular Entertainment: A Guide to Information Sources.* Detroit: Gale, 1980.

Communication Arts Indexes and Periodicals

Communication Abstracts.

Humanities Index.

Speech Communication Abstracts.

American Cinematographer.
Art & Cinema.
Columbia Journalism Review.
Communication Quarterly.
Film Literature Quarterly.
Film Quarterly.
Journal of Communication.
The Journal of Popular Film.
Journalism History.
Journalism Quarterly.
Quarterly Journal of Speech.

Computer Science Books

Anderson, R. G. *Dictionary of Data Processing and Computer Terms.* Philadelphia, PA: International Ideas, 1982.

Augarten, Stan. *Bit by Bit: An Illustrated History of Computers and Their Inventors.* New York: Ticknor & Fields, 1984.

Belzer, Jack, ed. *Encyclopedia of Computer Science and Technology.* New York: Dekker, 1975–1980.

Burton, Philip E. *A Dictionary of Minicomputing and Microcomputing.* New York: Garland Publishing Co., 1983.

Encyclopedia of Computer Science. New York: Petrocelli, 1976.

Encyclopedia of Cybernetics. New York: Barnes and Noble, 1968.

Godman, Arthur. *Barnes & Noble Thesaurus of Computer Science.* New York: Harper& Row, 1984.

Gore, Marvin R. *Computers and Information Systems.* 2nd ed. New York: McGraw, 1984.

A History of Computing in the Twentieth Century. Ed. N. Metropolis. San Diego, CA: Academic Press, 1980.

Kruzas, Anthony Thomas, ed. *Encyclopedia of Information Systems and Services.* 3rd ed. Detroit: Gale, 1978.

Lesko, Matthew. *The Computer Data and Database Sourcebook.* New York: Avon Books, 1984.

McGraw-Hill Encyclopedia of Electronics and Computers. New York: McGraw-Hill, 1983.

Pritchard, Alan. *A Guide to Computer Literature.* 2nd ed. Hamden, CT: Linnet Books, 1972.

Ralston, Anthony. *Encyclopedia of Computer Science and Engineering.* 2nd ed. New York: Van Nostrand Reinhold, 1982.

Rodgers, Harold A. *Funk & Wagnalls Dictionary of Data Processing Terms.* New York: Funk & Wagnalls, 1970.

Sippl, Charles J. *Computer Dictionary and Handbook.* 2nd ed. Indianapolis: Sams, 1972.

Computer Science Indexes and Periodicals

Computer Literature Index.
Computer and Control Abstracts.
Computer and Information Systems.
Computing Reviews.
Information Science Abstracts.
AT&T Bell Laboratories Technical Record.
Byte.
Communications of the Association for Computing Machinery.
Computer Methods in Applied Mechanics and Engineering.
Computer.
Computers and Education.
Creative Computing.
Data Management.
Data Processing.
Datamation.
EDP Analyzer.
IBM Journal of Research and Development.
IBM Systems Journal.
Information Sciences.
Information and Control.
Personal Computing.
Word Processing and Information Services.

Criminal Justice Books

Branham, Vernon C. *Encyclopedia of Criminology.* New York: Philosophical Library, 1949.

Chamelin, Neil C. *Introduction to Criminal Justice.* 2nd ed. New York: Prentice-Hall, 1979.

Cole, George F. *Major Criminal Justice Systems.* Beverly Hills, CA: Sage, 1981.

Cole, George F. *The American System of Criminal Justice.* 3rd ed. Monterey, CA: Brooks-Cole, 1982.

Crime and Punishment in America: A Historical Bibliography. Santa Barbara, CA: ABC-Clio, 1984.

Elsevier's Dictionary of Criminal Justice. Amsterdam: Elsevier, 1960.

Felknes, George T., and Harold K. Becker. *Law Enforcement: A Selected Bibliography.* 2nd ed. New York: Scarecrow Press, 1977.

Kadish, Sanford H., ed. *Encyclopedia of Crime and Justice.* New York: Macmillan, 1983.

Kinton, J. *Criminology and Criminal Justice in America: A Guide to the Literature.* Aurora, IL: Social Science and Sociological Resources, 1981.

O'Block, Robert J. *Criminal Justice Research Sources: A Guide to Criminal Justice Literature, Research and Sources of Data.* Cincinnati, OH: Anderson Publishing Co., 1983.

Radzinowicz, Leon. *Criminology and the Administration of Criminal Justice.* Westport, CT: Greenwood Press, 1976.

Rush, George Eugene. *Dictionary of Criminal Justice.* Boston: Holbrook Press, 1977.

Wright, Martin. *Use of Criminology Literature.* Hamden, CT: Archon Books, 1974.

Criminal Justice Indexes and Periodicals

Criminal Justice Abstracts.
Criminal Justice Periodicals Index.
American Criminal Law Review.
American Journal of Criminal Law.
The British Journal of Criminology.
Corrections Magazine.
Crime and Delinquency.
Crime and Social Justice.
Criminal Justice.
Criminal Justice Review
The Criminal Law Quarterly.
The Criminal Law Review.
Criminology.
Journal of Criminal Justice.
Journal of Research in Crime and Delinquency.

Police Studies.
Southern Journal of Criminal Justice.
Trial.

Education Books

Anderson, Scarvia B. *Encyclopedia of Educational Evaluation.* San Francisco: Josey-Bass, 1975.

Baatz, Charles Albert. *The Philosophy of Education: A Guide to Information Sources.* Detroit: Gale, 1980.

Berry, Dorothea M. *A Bibliographic Guide to Educational Research.* Metuchen, NJ: Scarecrow Press, 1975.

Encyclopedia of Education. Ed. Lee C. Deighton. New York: Macmillan, 1971.

Encyclopedia of Educational Research. Ed. Robert L. Ebel. 4th ed. New York: Macmillan, 1969.

Foskett, D. J. *How to Find Out: Educational Research.* New York: Pergamon, 1965.

Gage, Nathaniel Lees. *Handbook of Research on Teaching.* Chicago: Rand McNally, 1963.

Good, Carter V., ed. *Dictionary of Education.* 3rd ed. New York: McGraw-Hill, 1973.

Handbook of Adult Education. Ed. Robert M. Smith. 5th ed. New York: Macmillan, 1970.

Hillway, Tyrus. *Handbook of Educational Research.* Boston: Houghton, 1969.

The International Encyclopedia of Higher Education. Ed. Asa S. Knowles. San Francisco: Josey-Bass, 1977.

Kennedy, James R. *Library Research Guide to Education: Illustrated Search Strategy and Sources.* Ann Arbor, MI: Pieran Press, 1979.

Moore, Byron C. *A Dictionary of Special Education Terms.* Springfield, IL: Thomas, 1980.

Page, G. *International Dictionary of Education.* New York: Nichols, 1977.

Park, Joe, ed. *The Rise of American Education.* Evanston: Northwestern University Press, 1965.

Sedlak, Michael W. *American Educational History: A Guide to Information Sources.* Detroit: Gale, 1981.

Teacher's Encyclopedia. Englewood Cliffs, NJ: Prentice-Hall, 1966.

Unwin, Derick. *The Encyclopedia of Educational Media Communications and Technology.* London: Macmillan, 1979.

Education Indexes and Periodicals

Child Development Abstracts and Bibliography.
Current Index to Journals in Education.
Education Index.
Exceptional Child Education Resources.
Resources in Education.
Adult Education.
American Teacher.
Contemporary Education.
Education Digest.
Educational Forum.
Educational Leadership.
Educational Researcher.
Educational Technology.
Harvard Educational Review.
Instructor.
Journal of Education.
The Journal of Educational Research.
Journal of Reading.
The Journal of Special Education.
Phi Delta Kappan.
The Reading Teacher.

Engineering Books

Aviation/Space Dictionary. Ed. Ernest J. Gentle and Lawrence W. Reithmaier. 6th ed. Los Angeles: Aero, 1980.

Boone, Lalia Phipps. *The Petroleum Dictionary.* Norman: University of Oklahoma Press, 1952.

Brandrup, Johannes. *Polymer Handbook.* New York: Interscience, 1966.

Chemical Engineers' Handbook. 5th ed. New York: McGraw-Hill, 1973.

Chemical Technology: An Encyclopedic Treatment. New York: Barnes and Noble, 1968–73.

Civil Engineer's Reference Book. Ed. Leslie Spencer Blake. 3rd ed. London: Butterworths, 1975.

Cooke, Nelson Major. *Electronics and Nucleonics Dictionary.* 3rd ed. New York: McGraw-Hill, 1966.

Elsevier's Dictionary of Chemical Engineering. Amsterdam: Elsevier, 1968.

Encyclopedia of Chemical Technology. 2nd ed. New York: Interscience, 1963–70.

Encyclopedia of Engineering Materials and Processes. Ed. H. R. Claussen. New York: Reinhold, 1963.

Encyclopedia of Polymer Science and Technology. New York: Interscience, 1964–72.

Eshbach, O. W. *Handbook of Engineering Fundamentals.* 2nd ed. New York: Wiley, 1952.

Fluegge, Wilhelm. *Handbook of Engineering Mechanics.* New York: McGraw-Hill, 1962.

Hughes, Leslie. *Electronic Engineer's Reference Work.* 3rd ed. London: Hetwood, 1967.

Hunt, V. Daniel. *Energy Dictionary.* New York: Van Nostrand Reinhold, 1979.

Ireson, William Grant. *Handbook of Industrial Engineering and Management.* 2nd ed. Englewood Cliffs, NJ: Prentice-Hall, 1971.

Johnson, Allen J. *Fuels and Combustion Handbook.* New York: McGraw-Hill, 1951.

Jones, F. D. *Engineering Encyclopedia.* 3rd ed. New York: Industrial Press, 1963.

Lynch, Charles T., ed. *CRC Handbook of Materials Science.* Cleveland: CRC Press, 1974–75.

Mantell, Charles Letnam. *Engineering Materials Handbook.* New York: McGraw-Hill, 1958.

Markus, John. *Electronics Dictionary.* 4th ed. New York: McGraw-Hill, 1978.

Maynard, Harold Bright. *Industrial Engineering Handbook.* 3rd ed. New York: McGraw-Hill, 1971.

McGraw-Hill Encyclopedia of Energy. Ed. Daniel N. Lapedes. New York: McGraw-Hill, 1981.

McGraw-Hill Encyclopedia of Space. New York: McGraw-Hill, 1968.

Mount, Ellis. *Guide to Basic Information Sources in Engineering.* New York: Wiley, 1976.

Osbourne, Alan A. *Modern Maritime Engineer's Manual.* 2nd ed. New York: Conwell Maritime, 1965.

Perry, Robert H. *Engineering Manual.* 2nd ed. New York: McGraw-Hill, 1967.

Potter, James Harry. *Handbook of the Engineering Sciences.* Princeton, NJ: Nostrand, 1967.

Rothbart, Harold A. *Mechanical Design and Systems Handbook.* New York: McGraw-Hill, 1964.

Sarbacher, Robert Irving. *Encyclopedic Dictionary of Electronics and Nuclear Engineering.* Englewood Cliffs, NJ: Prentice-Hall, 1959.

Sounders, Mott. *Handbook of Engineering Fundamentals.* 3rd ed. New York: Wiley, 1975.

Standard Handbook for Civil Engineers. Ed. Frederick J. Merritt. 2nd ed. New York: McGraw-Hill, 1976.

Standard Handbook for Electrical Engineers. Ed. Donald G. Fink. 10th ed. New York: McGraw-Hill, 1968.

Thesaurus of Engineering and Scientific Terms. New York: Engineers Joint Council, 1967.

Use of Engineering Literature. Ed. K. W. Mildren. Boston: Butterworths, 1976.

Engineering Indexes and Periodicals

Applied Mechanics Reviews.
Applied Science and Technology Index.
Electrical and Electronics Abstracts.
Metals Abstracts.
American Society of Civil Engineers. Proceedings.
Aviation Week and Space Technology.
Building and Environment.
Chemical Engineer.
Chemical Engineering.
Civil Engineering.
Engineering.
International Journal of Engineering Science.
Journal of Engineering Materials and Technology.
Journal of Fluids Engineering.
Journal of Heat Transfer.
Journal of Structural Mechanics.
Mechanical Engineering.
Nuclear Technology.
Production Engineering.
Textile Research Journal.

Geography Books

Brewer, James Gordon. *The Literature of Geography: A Guide to Its Organization and Use.* 2nd ed. Hamden, CT: Linnet Books, 1978.

Columbia Lippencott Gazatteer of the World. Ed. Leon E. Seltzer. New York: Columbia University Press, 1962.

International Geographic Encyclopedia and Atlas. Boston: Houghton Mifflin, 1979.

Martinson, Tom L. *Introduction to Library Research in Geography.* Metuchen, NJ: Scarecrow, 1972.

Rand McNally Encyclopedia of World Rivers. Chicago: Rand McNally, 1980.

Schmeider, Allen A. *A Dictionary of Basic Geography.* Boston: Allyn & Bacon, 1970.

Stamp, Dudley. *Longmans Dictionary of Geography.* London: Longmans, 1966.

Webster's New Geographical Dictionary. Springfield, MA: Merriam, 1972.

Geography Indexes and Periodicals

Geo Abstracts.
Economic Geography.
Geographical Journal.
Geographical Review.
Geography.
Professional Geographer.

Geology Books

American Geological Institute. *Dictionary of Geological Terms.* Garden City, NY: Archon, 1976.

Challinor, John. *A Dictionary of Geology.* 5th ed. Oxford: Oxford University Press, 1978.

A Dictionary of Earth Sciences. Ed. Stella Steiger. New York: Pica, 1977.

The Encyclopedia of Paleontology. Stoudsburg, PA: Dowden, Hutchinson & Ross, 1979.

Fairbridge, Rhodes Whitmore, ed. *The Encyclopedia of Atmospheric Sciences and Astrogeology.* New York: Reinhold, 1967.

Fairbridge, Rhodes Whitmore. *The Encyclopedia of Geochemistry and Environmental Sciences.* New York: Van Nostrand Reinhold, 1972.

Fairbridge, Rhodes Whitmore. *The Encyclopedia of World Regional Geology.* Stroudsburg, PA: Dowden, Hutchinson and Ross, 1975.

Fenton, Carroll Lane. *The Fossil Book: A Record of Prehistoric Life.* Garden City, NY: Doubleday, 1958.

Fenton, Carroll Lane. *The Rock Book.* New York: Doubleday, 1940.

Gary, Margaret. *Glossary of Geology.* Washington: American Geological Institute, 1972.

Geikie, Archibald. *The Founders of Geology.* 2nd ed. New York: Dover, 1962.

Glossary of Meteorology. Ed. Ralph E. Huschke. Boston: American Meterological Society, 1959.

Groves, Donald G. *Ocean World Encyclopedia.* New York: McGraw-Hill, 1980.

Huxley, Anthony Julian. *Standard Encyclopedia of the World's Mountains.* New York: Putnam, 1962.

Kaplan, Stuart R., ed. *A Guide to Information Sources in Mining, Minerals and Geosciences.* New York: Interscience, 1965.

McGraw-Hill Encyclopedia of the Geological Sciences. New York: McGraw-Hill, 1978.

Nelson, Archibald and Kenneth Davies Nelson. *Dictionary of Applied Geology: Mining and Civil Engineering.* New York: Philosophical Library, 1967.

Pough, Frederick H. *A Field Guide to Rocks and Minerals.* 4th ed. Boston: Houghton Mifflin, 1976.

Shipley, Robert Morill. *Dictionary of Gems and Gemology.* 5th ed. Los Angeles: Gemological Institute of America, 1951.

Tver, David F. *The Petroleum Dictionary.* New York: Van Nostrand Reinhold, 1980.

U. S. Coast and Geodetic Survey. *Earthquake History of the United States.* Washington: GPO, 1965.

Visher, Stephen Sargent. *Climactic Atlas of the United States.* Cambridge: Harvard University Press, 1954.

Webster, Robert. *Gems: Their Sources, Description and Identification.* 3rd ed. Hamden, CT: Archon, 1975.

Wilson, David. *Geologic Names of North America.* Washington: GPO, 1959.

Wood, David Norris, ed. *Use of Earth Sciences Literature.* Hamden, CT: Archon Books, 1973.

Geology Indexes and Periodicals

Bibliography and Index of Geology.
General Science Index.
American Journal of Science.
American Mineralogist.
Chemical Geology.
Engineering Geology.
Geological Magazine.
Geological Society of America. Bulletin.
Journal of Geology.
Journal of Paleontology.
Modern Geology.

History Books

Adams, James Truslow. *Dictionary of American History.* 2nd ed. New York: Scribner, 1942–61.

American Historical Association. *Guide to Historical Literature.* New York: Macmillan, 1961.

Atlas of American History. Rev. ed. Ed. Kenneth T. Jackson. New York: Scribner's, 1978.

Barzun, Jacques, and Henry F. Graff. *The Modern Researcher.* 3rd ed. New York: Harcourt Brace Jovanovich, 1977.

Bickerman, Elian Joseph. *Chronology of the Ancient World.* Ithaca, NY: Cornell University Press, 1968.

Calmann, John. *Western Europe: A Handbook.* New York: Praeger, 1967.

The Cambridge Encyclopedia of Archaeology. Ed. Andrew Sherratt. New York: Crown, 1980.

Cambridge History of Africa. Ed. J. D. Fage. Cambridge: Cambridge University Press, 1978.

Cambridge Medieval History. New York: Macmillan, 1911–36.

Carruth, Gorton. *The Encyclopedia of American Facts and Dates.* 7th ed. New York: Crowell, 1979.

Champion, Sara. *A Dictionary of Terms and Techniques in Archaeology.* Oxford: Facts on File, 1980.

Day, Alan Edwin. *History: A Reference Handbook.* Hamden, CT: Linnet Books, 1977.

Dillon, Michael. *Dictionary of Chinese History.* London: Frank Cass, 1979.

The Encyclopedia of Southern History. Ed. David C. Roller. Baton Rouge: Louisiana State University Press, 1979.

Freidel, Frank, ed. *Harvard Guide to American History.* Cambridge: Harvard University Press, 1974.

Harper Encyclopedia of the Modern World. Ed. Richard B. Morris. New York: Harper, 1970.

Illustrated Encyclopedia of the Classical World. Ed. Michael Avi-Yonah and Israel Shatzman, New York: Harper and Row, 1975.

Keller, Helen Rex. *Dictionary of Dates.* New York: Macmillan, 1934.

Lane, Jack C. *America's Military Past: A Guide to Information Sources.* Detroit: Gale, 1980.

Langer, William Leonard. *The New Illustrated Encyclopedia of World History.* New York: H. N. Abrams, 1975.

Lanier, William Leonard. *An Encyclopedia of World History.* 5th ed. Boston: Houghton Mifflin, 1972.

Morison, Samuel Eliot. *The Oxford History of the American People.* New York: Oxford University Press, 1965.

Oxford History of England. Ed. George Clark. 2nd ed. Oxford: Clarendon Press, 1937–62.

Palmer, R. R., ed. *Atlas of World History.* Chicago: Rand McNally, 1965.

Powicke, Frederick Maurice. *Handbook of British Chronology.* 2nd ed. London: Royal Historical Society, 1961.

Shafer, Robert Jones, ed. *A Guide to Historical Method.* 3rd ed. Homewood, IL: Dorsey Press, 1980.

Steinberg, Sigfrid Heinrich. *Steinberg's Dictionary of British History.* 2nd ed. New York: St. Martin's, 1971.

The Times Atlas of World History. Ed. Geoffrey Barraclough. London: Times Books, 1978.

Webster's Guide to American History. Springfield, MA: Merriam, 1971.

History Indexes and Periodicals

America: History and Life.
Historical Abstracts.
Humanities Index.
American Heritage.
The American Historical Review.
Clio.

English Historical Review.
History and Theory.
History.
Journal of American History.
Journal of Economic History.
Journal of Medieval History.
The Journal of Medieval and Renaissance Studies.
Journal of Modern History.
Social History.

Home Economics Books

American Home Economics Association. *Handbook of Household Equipment Terminology.* 3rd ed. Washington: AHEA, 1970.

Association of Admistrators of Home Economics. *National Goals and Guidelines for Research in Home Economics.* East Lansing, MI: Michigan State University, 1970.

Bender, Arnold E. *Dictionary of Nutrition and Food Technology.* 2nd ed. Washington: Butterwort, 1965.

CRC Handbook of Food Additives. Ed. Thomas E. Furia. 2nd ed. Cleveland: Ccr Press, 1972.

East, Marjorie. *Home Economics: Past, Present, and Future.* Boston: Allyn & Bacon, 1980.

Encyclopedia of Textiles. 3rd ed. Englewood Cliffs, NJ: Prentice-Hall, 1980.

Gioello, Debbie Ann. *Fashion Production Terms.* New York: Fairchild Publications, 1979.

Glynn, Prudence. *In Fashion: Dress in the Twentieth Century.* New York: Oxford University Press, 1978.

Good Housekeeping. *Guide to Successful Homemaking.* New York: Harper, 1961.

Goodhart, Robert S. *Modern Nutrition in Health and Disease.* 6th ed. Philadelphia: Lea & Febiger, 1980.

Grotz, George. *The Current Antique Furniture Style and Price Guide.* Garden City, NY: Doubleday, 1979.

Montagne, Prosper. *Larousse Gastronomique: The Encyclopedia of Food, Wine and Cookery.* New York: Crown, 1961.

Patten, Marguerite. *Books for Cooks: A Bibliography of Cookery.* New York: Bowker, 1975.

Simon, Andre Louis, and Robin Howe. *Dictionary of Gastronomy.* New York: McGraw-Hill, 1970.

Sourcebook on Food and Nutrition. Chicago: Marquis Academic Media, 1978.

Wingate, Isabel B. *Fairchild's Dictionary of Textiles.* 6th ed. New York: Fairchild, 1979.

Yarwood, Doreen. *Encyclopedia of World Costume.* New York: Scribner, 1978.

Home Economics Indexes and Periodicals

Current Index to Journals in Education.
Education Index.
Nutrition Abstracts and Reviews.
Reader's Guide to Periodical Literature.
American Dietetic Association. Journal.
American Fabrics and Fashions.
American Home.
American Journal of Clinical Nutrition.
Better Decorating Ideas.
Better Homes and Gardens.
Canadian Home Economics Journal.
Costume.
Food Technology.
Food and Nutrition.
Furniture Design.
Home Economics Research Journal.
House and Garden.
Journal of Home Economics.
Journal of Nutrition Education.

Language Books

Baugh, Albert Croll. *A History of the English Language.* 2nd ed. New York: Appleton, 1957.

Bodmer, Frederick. *The Loom of Language.* Ed. Lancelot Hogben. New York: Norton, 1944.

Ducrot, Oswald. *Encyclopedia Dictionary of the Sciences of Language.* Baltimore: Johns Hopkins University Press, 1979.

Hartmann, R. R. K., and F. C. Stork. *Dictionary of Language and Linguistics.* New York: Wiley, 1972.

The Linguistic Atlas of England. Ed. Harold Orton. London: Croom Helm, 1978.

Pei, Mario Andrew. *Glossary of Linguistic Terminology.* New York: Columbia University Press, 1966.

Voegelin, Charles Frederick. *Classification and Index of the World's Languages.* New York: Elsevier, 1977.

Language Indexes and Periodicals

Language and Language Behavior Abstracts.

Language, Teaching and Linguistics.

MLA International Bibliography of Books and Articles on Modern Language and Literature.

American Journal of Philology.

Classical Philology.

General Linguistics.

International Journal of Americal Linguistics.

Journal of Linguistics.

Language of Society.

Modern Language Journal.

Verbatim.

Law Books

American Jurisprudence: A Modern Comprehensive Text Statement of American Law, State and Federal. 2nd ed. Rochester, NY: Lawyers Co-Operative, 1974–1978.

Bander, Edward J. *Legal Research and Education Abridgement.* Cambridge, MA: Ballinger, 1978.

Black, Henry Campbell. *Black's Law Dictionary.* 5th ed. St. Paul, MN: West Publishing Company, 1979.

Cohen, Morris L. *Legal Research in a Nutshell.* 3rd ed. St. Paul, MN: West Publishing Co., 1978.

Corpus Juris Secundum: *A Complete Restatement of the Entire American Law.* Brooklyn, NY: American Law Book Co., 1936–1974.

Encyclopedia Dictionary of Business Law. Englewood Cliffs, NJ: Prentice-Hall, 1961.

Honigsberg, Peter Jan. *Clueing into Legal Research.* Berkeley, CA: Golden Rain Press, 1979.

Jacobstein, J. Myron. *Fundamentals of Legal Research.* Mineola, NY: Foundation Press, 1977.

Kling, Samuel G. *The Complete Guide to Everyday Law.* 2nd ed. Chicago: Follett, 1970.

McCarrick, Earlean M. *U.S. Constitution: A Guide to Information Sources.* Detroit: Gale, 1980.

Price, Miles O. *Effective Legal Research.* 4th ed. Boston: Little, Brown, 1979.

Walker, David M. *The Oxford Companion to Law.* Oxford: Clarendon Press, 1980.

Law Indexes and Periodicals

Index to Legal Periodicals.
American Business Law Journal.
American Journal of Comparative Law.
Annual Survey of American Law.
Cambridge Law Journal.
Harvard Law Review.
Judicature.
Law Quarterly Review.
Law and Contemporary Problems.
Trial.
Yale Law Journal.

Literature Books

Altick, Richard Daniel, and Andrew Wright. *Selective Bibliography for the Study of English and American Literature.* 6th ed. New York: Macmillan, 1979.

Bartlett, John. *Familiar Quotations.* 15th ed. Ed. Emily Morison Beck. Boston: Little, Brown, 1980.

Bateson, Frederick Wilse, and Harrison T. Meserole. *A Guide to English and American Literature.* 3rd ed. London: Longman, 1976.

Beckson, Karl. *Literary Terms: A Dictionary.* New York: Farrar, Straus & Giroux, 1975.

Bell, Inglis Freeman, and Donald Baird. *The English Novel, 1578–1956: A Checklist of Twentieth-Century Criticisms.* Denver: Alan Swallow, 1959.

Black American Writers: Bibliographical Essays. Ed. M. Thomas Inge. New York: St. Martin's Press, 1978.

Cambridge History of American Literature. New York: Putnam, 1917–21.

Cambridge History of English Literature. Ed. A. W. Ward and A. R. Waller. Cambridge: Cambridge University Press, 1907–33.

Clareson, Thomas D. *Science Fiction Criticism: An Annotated Checklist.* Kent, Ohio: Kent State University Press, 1972.

Cline, Gloria Stark, and Jeffrey A. Baker. *An Index of Criticism of British and American Poetry.* Metuchen, NJ: Scarecrow, 1973.

Columbia Dictionary of Modern European Literature. 2nd ed. New York: Columbia University Press, 1980.

Contemporary Authors: A Bio-Bibliographical Guide to Current Authors and Their Works. Detroit: Gale, 1962.

Contemporary Poets. 3rd ed. Ed. James Vinson. New York: St. Martin's Press, 1980.

Cook, Dorothy Elizabeth. *Short Story Index.* New York: Wilson, 1953.

The Critical Temper: A Survey of Modern Criticism on English and American Literature from the Beginnings to the Twentieth Century. Ed. Martin Tucker. New York: Ungar, 1969.

Deutsch, Babette. *Poetry Handbook.* New York: Funk & Wagnalls, 1974.

Dictionary of Literary Biography. Detroit: Gale, 1978–80.

Eagle, Dorothy, and Hilary Carnell. *The Oxford Literary Guide to the British Isles.* Oxford: Clarendon Press, 1977.

Encyclopedia of Poetry and Poetics. Ed. Alex Preminger. Princeton, NJ: Princeton University Press, 1965.

Fleay, Frederick Gard. *Biographical Chronicle of the English Drama, 1559–1642.* New York: Franklin, 1962.

Gohdes, Clarence. *Bibliographical Guide to the Study of the Literature of the U.S.A.* 3rd ed. Durham, NC: Duke University Press, 1970.

Granger, Edith. *Granger's Index to Poetry.* 6th ed. New York: Columbia University Press, 1973.

Hart, James David. *The Oxford Companion to American Literature.* 4th ed. New York: Oxford University Press, 1965.

Harvey, Paul. *The Oxford Companion to English Literature.* 4th ed. Ed. Dorothy Eagle. Oxford: Clarendon Press, 1967.

Holman, Clarence Hugh. *A Handbook to Literature.* 4th ed. Indianapolis: Bobbs-Merrill, 1980.

Keller, Dean H. *Index to Plays in Periodicals.* Rev. ed. Metuchen, NJ: Scarecrow Press, 1979.

Klinck, Carl Frederick, ed. *Literary History of Canada.* Toronto: University of Toronto Press, 1965.

Leary, Lewis Gaston. *Articles on American Literature.* Durham, NC: Duke University Press, 1954–67.

Leary, Lewis, *American Literature: A Study and Research Guide.* New York: St. Martin's Press, 1976.

Leary, Lewis. *Articles on American Literature, 1968–1975.* Durham, NC: Duke University Press, 1979.

Longaker, John Mark, and Edwin Courtlandt Bolles. *Contemporary English Literature.* New York: Appleton, 1953.

Magill, Frank N. *Cyclopedia of Literary Characters.* New York: Harper, 1963.

Magill, Frank N. *Magill's Bibliography of Literary Criticism.* Englewood Cliffs, NJ: Salem Press, 1979.

Magill, Frank N. *Magill's Quotations in Context.* New York: Harper, 1966.

Malkoff, Karl. *Crowell's Handbook of Contemporary American Poetry.* New York: T. Y. Crowell, 1973.

McGraw-Hill Encyclopedia of World Drama. New York: McGraw-Hill, 1972.

Meserve, Walter J. *American Drama to 1900: A Guide to Information Sources.* Detroit: Galle, 1980.

Moulton, Charles Wells. *Library of Literary Criticism of English and American Authors Through the Beginning of the Twentieth Century.* New York: Ungar, 1966.

The New Cambridge Bibliography of English Literature. Cambridge: Cambridge University Press, 1969–74.

Nicoll, Allardyce. *A History of English Drama, 1660–1900.* Cambridge: Cambridge University Press, 1952–59.

The Oxford Dictionary of Quotations. 3rd ed. Oxford: Oxford University Press, 1979.

Oxford History of English Literature. Ed. Frank Percy Wilson and Bonamy Dobree. Oxford: Clarendon Press, 1945–69.

Schwartz, Nanda Lacey. *Articles on Women Writers: A Bibliography.* Santa Barbara, CA: ABC-Clio, 1977.

The Science Fiction Encyclopedia. Ed. Peter Nicholls. Garden City, NY: Dolphin Books, 1979.

Shaw, Harry. *Dictionary of Critical Terms.* New York: McGraw-Hill, 1972.

Southern Writers: A Biographical Dictionary. Ed. Robert Bain, Joseph M. Flora and Louis D. Rubin. Baton Rouge: Louisiana State University Press, 1979.

Spiller, Robert E. *Literary History of the United States.* 4th ed. New York: Macmillan, 1974.

Story, Norah. *The Oxford Companion to Canadian History and Literature.* Toronto: Oxford University Press, 1967.

Temple, Ruth Zabriskie, and Martin Tucker. *Twentieth Cen-*

tury British Literature: A Reference Guide and Bibliography. New York: Ungar, 1968.

    Walker, Warren S. *Twentieth-Century Short Story Explication.* 2nd ed. Hamden, CT: Shoe String Press, 1967.

    Woodress, James Leslie. *American Fiction, 1900–1950: A Guide to Information Sources.* Detroit: Gale, 1974.

Literature Indexes and Periodicals

Abstracts of English Studies.

Humanities Index.

MLA International Bibliography of Books and Articles on Modern Language and Literature.

American Literature.

Ariel.

Comparative Literature.

Critical Quarterly.

Criticism.

ELH (English Literary History).

Eighteenth Century Studies.

Essays in Criticism.

The Explicator.

Journal of American Studies.

Journal of Modern Literature.

MLN (Modern Language Notes).

Modern Fiction Studies.

Nineteenth Century Fiction.

Novel.

PMLA.

Review of English Studies.

The Southern Literary Journal.

Speculum.

Studies in English Literature 1500–1900.

Studies in Short Fiction.

Studies in the Novel.

Twentieth Century Literature.

Victorian Studies.

Mathematics Books

Burington, Richard Stevens. *Handbook of Mathematical Tables and Formulas.* 5th ed. New York: McGraw-Hill, 1973.

Burington, Richard Stevens. *Handbook of Probability and Statistics.* 2nd ed. New York: McGraw-Hill, 1970.

CRC Handbook of Mathematical Sciences. Ed. William H. Beyer. 5th ed. West Palm Beach, FL: CRC Press, 1978.

Dick, Ellie M. *Current Information Sources in Mathematics.* Littleton, CO: Libraries Unlimited, 1973.

Dorling, Alison Rosemary, ed. *Use of Mathematical Literature.* Woburn, MA: Butterworths, 1977.

Handbook of Tables for Mathematics. 4th ed. Cleveland, OH: Chemical Rubber Co., 1970.

International Dictionary of Applied Mathematics. Ed. W. F. Fresberger. Princeton: Van Nostrand, 1960.

International Encyclopedia of Statistics. Ed. William H. Kruskal. New York: Free Press, 1978.

James, Glenn, and Robert C. James. *Mathematics Dictionary.* 4th ed. New York: Van Nostrand, 1976.

Merritt, Frederick J. *Mathematics Manual: Methods and Principles of the Various Branches of Mathematics for Reference, Problem Solving and Review.* New York: McGraw-Hill, 1962.

Parke, Nathan Grier. *Guide to the Literature of Mathematics and Physics.* 2nd ed. New York: Dover, 1958.

Sneddon, Ian Naismith, ed. *Encyclopedic Dictionary of Mathematics for Engineers and Applied Scientists.* New York: Pergamon Press, 1976.

Universal Encyclopedia of Mathematics. New York: Simon and Schuster, 1964.

Mathematics Indexes and Periodicals

Current Mathematical Publications.
Mathematical Reviews.
Advances in Mathematics.
American Journal of Mathematics.
American Mathematical Society. Proceedings.
American Statistical Association. Journal.
Arithmetic Teacher.
Duke Mathematical Journal.

Journal for Research in Mathematics Education.
Journal of Recreational Mathematics.
Mathematics Magazine.

Medicine Books

American Medical Association. *Current Medical Information and Terminology.* 4th ed. Chicago: American Medical Association, 1971.

Black's Medical Dictionary. Ed. William A. R. Thompson. 31st ed. New York: Barnes and Noble, 1976.

Boucher, Carl O. *Current Clinical Dental Terminology.* St. Louis: Mosby, 1974.

Dorland's Illustrated Medical Dictionary. 24th ed. Philadelphia: Saunders, 1965.

Garrison, Fielding Hudson. *Introduction to the History of Medicine.* 4th ed. Philadelphia: Saunders, 1929.

Grad, Frank P. *Public Health Law Manual.* New York: American Public Health Association, 1970.

Hansen, Helen F. *Encyclopedic Guide to Nursing.* New York: McGraw-Hill, 1957.

Lunin, Lois F. *Health Sciences and Services: A Guide to Information Sources.* Detroit: Gale, 1979.

Mettler, Frederick Albert. *The Medical Sourcebook. Boston: Little, Brown 1959.*

Miller, Benjamin Frank. *Encyclopedia and Dictionary of Medicine, Nursing and Allied Health.* 2nd ed. Philadelphia: Saunders, 1978.

Morton, Leslie Thomas. *How to Use a Medical Library.* 6th ed. London: Heinemann Medical Books, 1979.

Physician's Desk Reference to Pharmaceutical Specialties and Biologicals. Rutherford, NJ: Medical Economics, 1946.

Roper, Fred. *Introduction to Reference Sources in Health Sciences.* Chicago: Medical Library Association, 1980.

Rosen, George. *A History of Public Health.* New York: M. D. Publishers, 1958.

Stedman, Thomas Lathrop. *Stedman's Medical Dictionary.* 23rd ed. Baltimore: Williams & Wilkins, 1976.

Stewart, Israel Maitland. *A History of Nursing from Ancient to Modern Times.* 5th ed. New York: Putnam, 1962.

Strauch, Katina P. *Guide to Library Resources for Nursing.* New York: Appleton-Century-Crofts, 1980.

Medicine Indexes and Periodicals

Cumulative Index to Nursing and Allied Health Literature.
Hospital Abstracts.
Hospital Literature Index.
Index Medicus.
American Heart Journal.
American Journal of Nursing.
American Journal of Obstetrics and Gynecology.
American Medical Association. Journal.
Annals of Internal Medicine.
Circulation.
International Nursing Review.
JOGN Nursing.
Journal of Pediatrics.
Journal of Practical Nursing.
Lancet.
New England Journal of Medicine.
Nursing Forum.

Music Books

Apel, Willi. *Harvard Dictionary of Music.* 2nd ed. Cambridge: Harvard University Press, 1969.

Baker, Theodore. *Baker's Biographical Dictionary of Musicians.* 6th ed. New York: Schirmer Books, 1978.

Britannica Book of Music. Ed. Benjamin Hadley. New York: Doubleday, 1980.

Case, Brian. *The Illustrated Encyclopedia of Jazz.* London: Salamander Books, 1978.

Davies, J. H. *Musicalia: Sources of Information in Music.* 2nd ed. Oxford: Pergamon, 1969.

The Encyclopedia of Jazz. New York: Horizon Press, 1960.

The Encyclopedia of Opera. Ed. Leslie Orrey. New York: Scribner, 1976.

Ewen, David. *Complete Book of the American Musical Theatre.* New York: Holt, 1958.

Ewen, David. *Encyclopedia of the Opera.* New York: Hill and Wang, 1963.

Fink, Robert. *Language of Twentieth Century Music: A Dictionary of Terms.* New York: Schirmer Books, 1975.

Fold, James J. *The Book of World-Famous Music: Classical, Popular and Folk.* New York: Crown, 1971.

Haydon, Glen. *Introduction to Musicology.* New York: Prentice-Hall, 1941.

Jackson, Irene V. *Afro-American Religious Music.* Westport, CT: Greenwood Press, 1979.

LePage, Jane Weiner. *Women Composers, Conductors and Musicians of the Twentieth Century.* Metuchen, NJ: Scarecrow Press, 1980.

Marcuse, Sibly. *Musical Instruments: A Comprehensive Dictionary.* Garden City, NY: Doubleday, 1964.

Martin, George Whitner. *The Opera Companion to Twentieth-Century Opera.* New York: Dodd, Mead & Co., 1979.

The New Grove Dictionary of Music and Musicians. Ed. Stanley Sadie. London: Macmillan, 1980.

New Oxford History of Music. London: Oxford University Press, 1954–73.

Picerno, Vincent J. *Dictionary of Musical Terms.* Brooklyn: Haskell House, 1976.

Randel, Don Michael. *Harvard Concise Dictionary of Music.* Cambridge, MA: Belknap Press, 1978.

Rosenthal, Harold D. *The Concise Oxford Dictionary of Opera.* 2nd ed. London: Oxford University Press, 1979.

Scholes, Percy Alfred. *The Oxford Companion to Music.* 10th ed. London: Oxford University Press, 1970.

Thompson, Oscar. *The International Cyclopedia of Music and Musicians.* 9th ed. New York: Dodd, 1964.

Vinton, John, ed. *Dictionary of Contemporary Music.* New York: Dutton, 1974.

Music Indexes and Periodicals

Jazz Index.
Music Index.
American Choral Review.
Clavier.
Early Music.
The Hymn.
Instrumentalist.

Journal of Church Music.
Journal of Jazz Studies.
Journal of Research in Music Education.
Music Journal.
The Musical Quarterly.
Opera.
Perspectives of New Music.
The Strad.
Tempo.
The World of Music.

Philosophy Books

Baldwin, James Mark. *Dictionary of Philosophy and Psychology.* New York: Macmillan, 1901–05.

Bertman, Martin A. *Research Guide in Philosophy.* Morristown, NJ: General Learning Press, 1974.

Borchardt, Dietrich Hans. *How to Find Out in Philosophy and Psychology.* Oxford: Pergamon, 1968.

DeGeorge, Richard T. *A Guide to Philosophical Bibliography and Research.* New York: Appleton-Century-Crofts, 1971.

DeGeorge, Richard T. *The Philosopher's Guide to Sources, Research Tools, Professional Life and Related Fields.* Lawrence: Regents Press of Kansas, 1980.

Dictionary of the History of Ideas. Ed. Philip P. Wiener. New York: Scribner's, 1973–74.

Encyclopedia of Philosophy. Ed. Paul Edwards. New York: Macmillan, 1967.

Handbook of World Philosophy: Contemporary Developments Since 1945. Ed. John R. Burr. Westport, CT: Greenwood Press, 1980.

Lacey, Alan Robert. *A Dictionary of Philosophy.* London: Routledge and Kegan Paul, 1976.

Reese, William L. *Dictionary of Philosophy and Religion: Eastern and Western Thought.* Atlantic Highlands, NJ: Humanities Press, 1980.

Tobey, Jeremy L. *The History of Ideas.* Santa Barbara, CA: Clio Books, 1975–76.

Urmson, James Opie, ed. *The Concise Encyclopedia of Western Philosophy and Philosophers.* 2nd ed. London: Hutchinson, 1975.

Philosophy Indexes and Periodicals

The Philosopher's Index.
American Philosophical Quarterly.
Inquiry.
International Philosophical Quarterly.
Journal of Philosophical Logic.
Journal of Philosophy.
Journal of the History of Philosophy.
Mind.
Philosophical Books.
Philosophical Quarterly.
Philosophical Review.
Philosophy of Science.

Physics Books

Condon, E. U. *Handbook of Physics.* 2nd ed. New York: McGraw-Hill, 1967.

Encyclopedia Dictionary of Physics. London: Pergamon, 1961–64.

Encyclopedia of Physics. Reading, MA: Addison-Wesley, 1981.

The Facts on File Dictionary of Physics. 2nd ed. Ed. John Daintith. New York: Facts on File, 1981.

Gray, Harold James and Alan Isaacs, eds. *A New Dictionary of Physics.* New York: Longman, 1975.

Handbook of Optics. Ed. Walter G. Driscoll. New York: McGraw-Hill, 1978.

Menzel, Donald Howard, ed. *Fundamental Formulas of Physics.* New York: Dover, 1960.

Michaels, Walter C., ed. *International Dictionary of Physics and Electronics.* Princeton, NJ: Van Nostrand, 1961.

Parke, Nathan Grier. *Guide to the Literature of Mathematics and Physics, Including Related Works on Engineering Science.* 2nd ed. New York: Dover, 1958.

Thewlis, James. *Concise Dictionary of Physics and Related Subjects.* Oxford: Pergamon, 1973.

Whitford, Robert Henry. *Physics Literature: A Reference Manual.* 2nd ed. Metuchen, NJ: Scarecrow, 1968.

Physics Indexes and Periodicals

Current Physics Index.
General Science Index.
Physics Abstracts.
American Journal of Physics.
Annals of Physics.
Applied Optics.
Astronomy.
Chemical Physics.
Comments on Modern Physics.
Foundations of Physics.
Journal for the History of Astronomy.
Journal of Applied Physics.
Journal of Chemical Physics.
Journal of Mathematical Physics.
Journal of Physics.
Modern Astronomy.
Nuclear Physics.
Physical Review.
Physics Today.

Political Science Books

Book of the States, Chicago: Council of State Governments, 1935.

Brock, Clifton. *The Literature of Political Science.* New York: Bowker, 1969.

Gallup, George Horace. *The Gallup Poll: Public Opinion, 1935–1971.* New York: Random House, 1972.

Greenstein, Fred I. *Handbook of Political Science.* Reading, MA: Addison-Wesley, 1975.

Holler, Frederick L. *The Information Sources of Political Science.* 2nd ed. Santa Barbara, CA: ABC-Clio, 1975.

Kurian, George Thomas. *Encyclopedia of the Third World.* New York: Facts on File, 1978.

Lagueur, Walter Ze'ev, ed. *A Dictionary of Politics.* Rev. ed. New York: Free Press, 1974.

Murphy, Thomas P. *Urban Politics: A Guide to Information Sources.* Detroit: Gale, 1978.

Pfaltzgraff, Robert L. *The Study of International Relations: A Guide to Information Sources.* Detroit: Gale, 1977.

Plano, Jack C. *The American Political Dictionary.* 3rd ed. Hinsdale, IL: Dryden Press, 1972.

Political Handbook and Atlas of the World. New York: Harper and Row, 1927.

Rouse, John Edward. *Public Administration in America: A Guide to Information Sources.* Detroit: Gale, 1980.

Safire, William L. *Safire's Political Dictionary.* New York: Random House, 1978.

Smith, Edward C. *Dictionary of American Politics.* 2nd ed. New York: Barnes and Noble, 1968.

Worldmark Encyclopedia of the Nations. Ed. Moshe Y. Sachs. 4th ed. New York: Worldmark Press, 1971.

Political Science Indexes and Periodicals

ABC Pol Sci: Advance Bibliography of Contents, Political Science and Government.

Public Affairs Information Service.

Sage Public Administration Abstracts.

American Journal of Political Science.

American Political Science Review.

Annals of the American Academy of Political and Social Science.

The Atlantic Community Quarterly.

CQ Weekly Report.

Comparative Politics.

Congressional Digest.

Current History.

Foreign Affairs.

The Journal of Politics.

Political Studies.

Publius.

World Politics.

Psychology Books

Alexander, Franz Gabriel. *The History of Psychiatry.* New York: Harper, 1966.

American Psychiatric Association. *A Psychiatric Glossary.* 4th ed. New York: Basic Books, 1975.

Bell, James E. *A Guide to Library Research in Psychology.* Dubuque, IA: W. C. Brown, 1971.

Buros, Oscar Krisen, ed. *Mental Measurements Yearbook.* Highland Park, NJ: Gryphon, 1938.

Campbell, Robert Jean. *Psychiatric Dictionary.* 5th ed. New York: Oxford University Press, 1981.

Chaplin, James Patrick. *Dictionary of Psychology.* New York: Dell, 1975.

Drever, James. *A Dictionary of Psychology.* Baltimore: Penguin, 1964.

Encyclopedia of Mental Health. New York: Watts, 1963.

Encyclopedia of Occultism and Parapsychology. Ed. Leslie Shepard. Detroit: Gale, 1978.

Encyclopedia of Psychology. New York: Herder and Herder, 1972.

English, Horace Bidwell. *A Comprehensive Dictionary of Psychological and Psychoanalytical Terms: a Guide to Usage.* New York: Longman, 1958.

Greenberg, Bette. *How to Find Out in Psychiatry.* New York: Pergamon, 1978.

Hinsie, Leland Earl. *Psychiatric Dictionary.* 4th ed. New York: Oxford University Press, 1970.

Psychology Indexes and Periodicals

Psychological Abstracts.
American Psychologist.
Contemporary Psychology.
Developmental Psychology.
Journal of Abnormal Psychology.
Journal of Applied Psychology.
Journal of Behavior Processes.
Journal of Comparative and Physiological Psychology.
Journal of Consulting and Clinical Psychology.

Journal of Counseling Psychology.
Journal of Educational Psychology.
Journal of Experimental Psychology.
Journal of Personality and Social Psychology.
Professional Psychology.
Psychological Bulletin.
Psychological Review.
Psychology Today.

Recreation Books

The Baseball Encyclopedia: The Complete and Official Guide to Major League Baseball. Ed. Joseph L. Reichler. 4th ed. New York: Macmillan, 1979.

Besford, Pat. *Encyclopedia of Swimming.* New York: St. Martin's Press, 1971.

Cuddon, John A. *The International Dictionary of Sports and Games.* New York: Schocken Books, 1980.

Cummings, Parke. *The Dictionary of Sports.* New York: Barnes, 1949.

Diagram Group. *Rules of the Game.* New York: Paddington Press, 1974.

The Encyclopedia of Crafts. Ed. Laura Torbet. New York: Scribners, 1980.

Encyclopedia of Physical Education, Fitness and Sports. Ed. Thomas K. Cureton, Reading, MA: Addison-Wesley, 1977.

Encyclopedia of Sailing. New York: Harper & Row, 1978.

Evans, Webster. *Encyclopedia of Golf.* New York: St. Martin's Press, 1971.

Farquhar, Carley. *The Sportsman's Almanac.* New York: Harper, 1965.

Henshaw, Richard. *The Encyclopedia of World Soccer.* Washington: New Republic Books, 1979.

Hickock, Ralph. *New Encyclopedia of Sports.* New York: McGraw-Hill, 1977.

Hollander, Zander. *The Modern Encyclopedia of Basketball.* 2nd ed. Garden City, NY: Dolphin Books, 1979.

Menke, Frank G. *The Encyclopedia of Sports.* 6th ed. South Brunswick, NJ: A. S. Barnes, 1978.

Murdoch, Joseph S. F. *Golf: A Guide to Information Sources.* Detroit: Gale, 1979.

Norback, Craig T. *The New American Guide to Athletics, Sports, and Recreation.* New York: New American Library, 1979.

Robertson, Maxwell. *The Encyclopedia of Tennis.* New York: Viking, 1974.

Sunnucks, Anne. *The Encyclopedia of Chess.* 2nd ed. London: Hale, 1976.

Turkin, Hy. *The Official Encyclopedia of Baseball.* 9th ed. South Brunswick, NJ: A. S. Barnes, 1977.

U. S. Lawn Tennis Association. *Official Encyclopedia of Tennis.* New York: Harper, 1972.

Recreation Indexes and Periodicals

Physical Education Index.
Athletic Journal.
Baseball Digest.
Basketball Digest.
Bowling Magazine.
Coach and Athlete.
Golf Digest.
Journal of Leisure Research.
Journal of Physical Education and Recreation.
Journal of Physical Education.
Journal of Sport History.
Runner's World.
Sport and Recreation.
Sports Illustrated.
Swimming World.
Tennis.

Religion Books

Adams, Charles Joseph, ed. *A Reader's Guide to the Great Religions.* 2nd ed. New York: Free Press, 1977.

Allmen, Jean Jacques von. *A Companion to the Bible.* New York: Oxford University Press, 1958.

Anderson, Charles S. Augsburg *Historical Atlas of Christianity in the Middle Ages and Reformation.* Minneapolis: Augsburg, 1967.

Blair, Edward P. *Abingdon Bible Handbook.* Nashville: Abingdon Press, 1975.

Bollier, John A. *The Literature of Theology.* Philadelphia: Westminster Press, 1979.

Douglas, James Dixon, ed. *The New International Dictionary of the Christian Church.* Grand Rapids, MI: Zondervan, 1974.

Douglas, James Dixon. *The New International Dictionary of the Christian Church.* Rev. ed. Grand Rapids, MI: Zondervan, 1978.

Encyclopedic Dictionary of Religion. Ed. Paul K. Meagher. Washington: Corpus Publications. 1979.

Encyclopedic Dictionary of the Bible. New York: McGraw-Hill, 1963.

Encyclopedia Judaica. New York: Macmillan, 1972.

Encyclopedia of Religion and Ethics. Ed. James Hastings. New York: Scribners, 1908–27.

Farmer, David Hugh. *The Oxford Dictionary of Saints.* Oxford: Clarendon Press, 1978.

Ferguson, John. *An Illustrated Encyclopedia of Mysticism and the Mystery Religions.* London: Thames and Hudson, 1977.

Hardon, John A. *Modern Catholic Dictionary.* Garden City, NY: Doubleday, 1980.

The Interpreter's Dictionary of the Bible. New York: Abingdon, 1962.

Kennedy, James R. *Library Research Guide to Religion and Theology.* Ann Arbor, MI: Pieron Press, 1974.

Mayer, Frederick Emanual. *The Religious Bodies of America.* 2nd ed. St. Louis: Concordia, 1956.

Mead, Frank Spencer. *Handbook of Denominations in the United States.* 7th ed. Nashville: Abingdon, 1980.

Melton, J. Gordon. *The Encyclopedia of American Religions.* Wilmongton, NC: McGrath, 1978.

New Catholic Encyclopedia. New York: McGraw-Hill, 1967.

The Oxford Dictionary of the Christian Church. Ed. F. L. Cross and G. A. Livingstone. 2nd ed. London: Oxford University Press, 1974.

Schaff, Philip. *History of the Christian Church.* New York: Scribner, 1889–1910.

Religion Indexes and Periodicals

Christian Periodical Index.

Humanities Index.

Index to Religious Periodical Literature.

Christian Herald.
Christianity Today.
Church History.
History of Religions.
Harvard Theological Review.
Journal of Biblical Literature.
Journal of Ecumenical Studies.
Religious Education.
Theology Today.

Sociology Books

Bart, Pauline. *The Student Sociologist's Handbook.* 3rd ed. Glenview, IL: Scott, Foresman, 1981.

Bergman, Peter M. *The Chronological History of the Negro in America.* New York: Harper, 1969.

Burke, Joan Martin. *Civil Rights.* 2nd ed. New York: Bowyer, 1974.

Coon, C. S. *The Origin of Races.* New York: Knopf, 1962.

Death Education: An Annotated Resource Guide. Washington: Hemisphere Publishing Corporation, 1980.

Dictionary of American Penology: An Introductory Guide. Westport, CT: Greenwood Press, 1979.

Edwards, Willie M. *Gerontology: A Core List of Significant Works.* Ann Arbor, MI: Institute of Gerontology, 1978.

Encyclopedia of Anthropology. Ed. David E. Hunter and Philip Whitten. New York: Harper & Row, 1976.

Encyclopedia of Black America. Ed. W. Augustus Low. New York: McGraw-Hill, 1981.

Encyclopedia of Sociology. Guilford, CT: Duskin Publishing Group, 1974.

Family Factbook. Chicago: Marquis Academic Media, 1978.

Frantz, Charles. *The Student Anthropologist's Handbook.* Cambridge, Mass: Schenkman, 1972.

Gould, Julius, ed. *A Dictionary of the Social Sciences.* New York: Free Press, 1964.

Handbook of American Popular Culture. Ed. Thomas Inge. Westport, CT: Greenwood Press, 1978–80.

Handbook of Contemporary Developments in World Sociology. Raj P. Mohan, ed. Westport, CT: Greenwood Press, 1975.

Harvard Encyclopedia of American Ethnic Groups. Ed. Stephen Thernstrom. Cambridge, MA: Harvard University Press, 1980.

Hauser, Philip Morris, ed. *Handbook for Social Research in Urban Areas.* Paris: UNESCO, 1965.

Heath, Dwight B. *Alcohol Use and World Cultures.* Toronto: Addiction Research Foundation, 1981.

History of the Family and Kinship. Ed. Gerald L. Soliday. Millwood, NY: Kraus International Publications, 1980.

Honigman, John J. *Handbook of Social and Cultural Anthropology.* Chicago: Rand McNally, 1973.

Hoover, Dwight W. *Cities.* New York: Bowker, 1976.

Hoult, Thomas Ford. *Dictionary of Modern Sociology.* Totowa, NJ: Littlefield, Adams, 1969.

International Handbook on Aging. Ed. Erdman Palmore. Westport, CT: Greenwood Press, 1980.

Krogman, Wilton Marion. *A Bibliography of Human Morphology, 1914–1939.* Chicago: University of Chicago Press, 1941.

Lester, David. *Suicide: A Guide to Information Sources.* Detroit: Gale, 1980.

Lynn, Naomi B. *Research Guide in Women's Studies.* Morristown, NJ: General Learning Press, 1974.

Milden, James Wallace. *The Family in Past Time: A Guide to the Literature.* New York: Garland, 1977.

Murphy, Thomas P. *Urban Indicators: A Guide to Information Sources.* Detroit: Gale, 1980.

Puerto Rican Research and Resources Center. *The Puerto Ricans: An Annotated Bibliography.* New York: Bowker, 1973.

Reference Encyclopedia of the American Indian. New York: B. Klein, 1967.

Robinson, Barbara J. *The Mexican American: A Critical Guide to Research Aids.* Greenwich, CT: JAI Press, 1980.

Young, Eric Fiske. *Dictionary of Social Welfare.* New York: Social Sciences, 1948.

Sociology Indexes and Periodicals

Public Affairs Information Service.

Social Sciences Index.

Sociological Abstracts.

Aging.

American Anthropologist.

American Behavioral Scientist.

American Ethnologist.
American Geriatrics Society Journal.
American Journal of Sociology.
American Sociological Review.
Anthropological Quarterly.
Clinical Social Work Journal.
Contemporary Sociology.
Current Anthropology.
Geriatrics.
International Journal of Comparative Sociology.
Journal of Gerontology.
Journal of Marriage and the Family.
Journal of Social Issues.
Public Welfare.
Rural Sociology.
Small Group Behavior.

INDEX

1 2 3 4 5 6 7 8 9 0